INDIGO HAUN⌐

INDIGO HAUNTED

Exciting sequel to the life-changing Indigo Awakes

Stephanie de Winter

A record of this publication is available from the British Library.

ISBN 978-1-907203-78-7

Typesetting by Wordzworth Ltd
www.wordzworth.com

Cover design by Titanium Design Ltd
www.titaniumdesign.co.uk

Printed by Lightning Source UK
www.lightningsource.com

Cover image by Anne Sophie Roux

Published by Local Legend
www.local-legend.co.uk

For James and Thomas C, Tara and Krystian S,
Tom Graham (Poppa) and to
my granddad Thomas Connolly.
With love. X

*"Action without vision is only passing time.
Vision without action is merely daydreaming.
But vision with action can change the world."*

Nelson Mandela

Acknowledgements

Tess Bourgenot, for being the face of Indigo.

Stephane Burton, Reiki Master and friend
full of wisdom and light.

Solara An-Ra, thank you for your valuable daily meditations.

Poet Joseph Williams, For the Love of Whisky.

Kay Johnson, for your support.

Nigel Peace at Local Legend, thank you for your vision,
hard work and dedication.

Tara and Krystian Smith, for your ideas and encouragement.

The seven archangels.

Freedom fighter, patriot and friend Marti Morrison,
always an inspiration.

And thanks to all of you who bought and read *Indigo Awakes*,
and for the positive response to my debut novel. Your support is
valuable and I appreciate it. I hope you enjoy *Indigo Haunted*.

About the Author

Stephanie de Winter lives in East Lothian.

Having discovered Reiki and begun to learn the art of spiritual healing, she writes about how to transform a life of abuse and depression into a true spiritual path.

Her heroine was introduced to us in her stunning debut novel *Indigo Awakes* and this is the eagerly anticipated and gripping action sequel.

www.stephaniedewinter.co.uk

Previous Publications

Indigo Awakes (Local Legend, ISBN 978-1-907203-44-2),
also available as an eBook

Contents

The Story So Far

Indigo Summers was going nowhere. She was tired and depressed. As conflict with both her partner and her employer grew, their increasing abuse was driving her life into chaos.

But then a quiet yet strong voice within began to demand change. She was visited at night by intense dreams, and synchronicities in her daily life showed her an alternative path... Indigo began a new journey into the unknown. She discovered Reiki healing which gave her the strength and determination to battle the demons of her past and to explore her own spirituality. She learned to have faith in herself and in a higher power.

Step by step her world was transformed. In a borrowed campervan she set off for the natural peace and beauty of the east coast of Scotland, where she met local policeman William MacLeod. As their friendship grew, Indigo decided to move to Scotland for a new beginning. It was a time to heal and to discover her true self.

Stephanie de Winter's stunning debut novel *Indigo Awakes* has inspired many to follow their own path. Beautifully written in simple language, with a narrative that every one of us can relate to, the author shows us a new way to live, free of fear and confusion.

As this sequel begins, Indigo has taken a room in the house of William's friend, Wallace. She is at peace. But she is about to discover that life is not that simple... Far greater and more terrifying challenges lie ahead.

ONE

The Shift Begins

Piano music rumbled through the house, vibrating ancient wooden floorboards hidden beneath thick cream carpet. The sleeping form of Indigo Summers stretched drowsily as Beethoven's Moonlight Sonata swirled around her. Sitting up in bed, she tried to focus through a blur of sleep at the small digits displayed on her mobile `phone. It was eleven o'clock in the morning. So late!

Red wine was the culprit. Although she drank most days, she usually carefully controlled the amount. Last night, however, she had spent a companionable evening with William MacLeod at the house where she rented rooms from his old friend Wallace. They had talked, drunk wine and danced together. Indigo smiled as she recalled the pleasant sensation of William's hard, fit body close to hers and the subtle scent of his aftershave. It had taken all her willpower to stagger off to bed alone, leaving him asleep on the sofa downstairs. She'd fallen asleep feeling happy and content, without bothering to draw the long ruby curtains.

Now rain lashed the French windows. The dull day was shrouded in grey fog as if some spiteful prankster had wiped paint from the beautiful scenic seascape outside, leaving behind a smeared and dreary blank canvas. Through half shut eyes she watched idly as rain streamed down the glass doors. Absorbing the music she dozed in and out of sleep feeling warm and lazy.

♦ ♦ ♦

William was sitting on the bed next to her. He was speaking to her but she couldn't hear what he was saying.

"Can't hear you," she tried to tell him but her lips were paralysed, her voice powerless and silent. Suddenly light illuminated the dull room and William's eyes darkened out of recognition. He uttered words in a foreign dialect asking her to pay attention. It was a thick accent that she thought might be Egyptian; she had lived there for a year when she was younger. Indigo watched as William transformed into the form of the old Egyptian gentleman she'd met fleetingly at the age of twenty-two.

He muttered the same words to her as he had twenty years before. It had been a bizarre event. Indigo was dining at an expensive roof terrace restaurant in Cairo with friends, when the man had walked past her table with another man of similar years, deep in conversation. He appeared not to have noticed her until he stopped and retraced his footsteps, standing in front of her and staring down with huge, dark, intelligent eyes. He had no wares to sell and asked for nothing. He was well dressed and looked respectable.

"Beware the wolf in sheep's clothing," he said.

Indigo had asked what he meant, glancing at her friends to see if they would get a similar prophecy but he just repeated himself and walked away with his confidant. He paid no attention to her companions. Her Egyptian friends had laughed, saying that Egypt was full of cranks fabricating falsehoods in order to extract money as their country was poor and had a virtually non-existent welfare state. However, he hadn't asked for money, nor looked ragged or malnourished. His words had entered her thoughts many times over the years.

Now he had revisited, seated in William's form. His black eyes burned into hers.

"Beware the wolf in sheep's clothing," he repeated in a timeless voice. Again she asked him for an interpretation, expecting him to say nothing, but this time he added, "The hunter is always in a guise, playing on weakness. The strong will not fall prey if they do not allow themselves to..."

◆ ◆ ◆

Indigo awoke abruptly feeling dehydrated, sweaty and fearful. The Egyptian's words had haunted her for years. Why had he returned now when she was finally carefree, happy and content? Why not before when life had been traumatic and chaotic? It made no sense. Damn him! It appeared that higher powers had even greater things planned for her and she would not be allowed to sit back and be complacent. It was a warning - but of what and why? Indigo had learned to accept the importance of messages and signs through dreams and synchronicities, so she could hardly dismiss this profound dream as rubbish just because it made her feel uncomfortable. Instead, she needed to acknowledge that it had been sent as an insight, a chance to prepare for darker times that were to follow.

Washing her face, she glanced at her pale reflection in the bathroom mirror.

"You *are* strong," she told her reflection. She'd made such progress over the past months. It had taken courage to move up to Scotland and embrace a new way of living. She was still healing from the abuse suffered at the hands of Mike, her ex-partner, and her employer. It took time to heal and her spirituality involved not just changing her whole way of thinking but also how she reacted to negative people and events. The dream was an example of that. Her first reaction had been fear and then anger that he had disrupted her happiness. This was a negative response. The positive thing to do was to embrace the message and be grateful for the warning and heed it in the months to come. Change was a tough path to travel but there was no turning back for her. She had progressed too far.

Applying make-up, she tiptoed downstairs to the kitchen. She would not dwell on the dream. William had a rare day off work and hinted that he wanted to spend it with her. Desperate for a cup of tea, she paused by Wallace's door wondering whether or not to ask him if he wanted a drink. The flawless piano music was coming from the lounge where they'd spent the previous evening. It was a sweet, melodious and calming sound. William hadn't mentioned that he played, but they were still getting to know each other.

"Didn't mean to sleep so late!" she laughed, walking into the lounge. The fire had been relit and yellow and purple flames beckoned to her, inviting her in. The room was warm and cosy.

The shiny mahogany grand piano situated at the far end of the room was partially obscured from view by tall green plants that stood behind the imposing red leather Chesterfield sofas crowding the fireplace. For a moment Indigo froze in confusion. The man seated at the piano was neither William nor Wallace.

He stopped playing and stood up.

"Hi. I'm Finn Cuthbert. Wallace's son... you must be Imogen. Dad's lodger and new pal. I've heard all about you." He smiled warmly and moved towards her, embracing her in a friendly hug.

"It's Indigo actually, but your Dad prefers Imogen, or thinks that's my name, not sure which." She extracted herself from his strong arms. Finn grinned. He was in his early forties, taller than William with thick blond hair that flopped over a strong face. His mouth was sensual and he'd inherited his father's bright blue twinkly eyes.

"The old fella's a bit on the deaf side in his right ear. Downside to being in the military for forty-odd years. He seems okay. I was worried that he'd really hurt himself when he fell recently. William called me about it. Good of him to let me know."

"Yes, that sounds like William," said Indigo. "You and he are friends?" They looked about the same age. She wondered where William was. He'd been asleep on the sofa when she'd left him. "I thought it was his day off?" she added.

"Yes, best pals but more like brothers. We get on but we fight too... William had to work. Wasn't very happy about it. Left as I was arriving. Don't know why he's wasting his time in the police." He raised his eyebrows. "Nice chap, William, but complicated. He's great with Dad. A better son to him than his actual son." Finn's voice was soft with the merest trace of a Scottish accent.

"I think he feels it's a worthwhile job," Indigo commented defensively. "Do you live locally, Finn?" William and Wallace had said little about him. Finn shook his head.

"Used to but I've been living in Italy for a while now. Lake Garda – Riva del Garda. I'm an artist. Not quite the career for the son of a naval officer. Dad didn't mind though." He smiled. "Sorry, I didn't mean to say that being a policeman was a crap job. It's just not what I expected for William."

"You don't sound very Scottish, Finn."

"I was educated at boarding school in England. You don't either."

"I was brought up in England. My parents are Scottish."

"How rude I must seem. Let me make you a cup of tea."

"I can make it if you like."

Finn suddenly seemed flustered. "No, let me."

He sauntered out to the kitchen. Dressed in dark jeans and a black silk shirt, a trail of expensive aftershave travelled on the breeze behind him. Indigo followed and sat perched on a stool by the breakfast island. The Aga was lit and the kitchen warm and cosy. She smiled as she watched Finn make the tea. Suddenly her life was saturated with good looking charismatic men. She grinned. Mike, even at his most positive, was out of his depth.

"Can I cook you breakfast? Or brunch?" He smiled as he glanced at the clock that now read midday.

"Brunch," Indigo laughed. "What did you have in mind?"

Finn rummaged in the depths of the fridge. Pulling out vegetarian bacon and eggs, he chuckled.

"There's no way these belong to Dad."

"Mine actually."

"Cool. I like veggie food too," said Finn. "Mind if I share?"

"Go ahead." Indigo accepted the mug of dark builder's tea Finn thrust at her. He seemed to enjoy being busy and she was beginning to feel a little hung over, so she let him cook without an argument. "So you flew back from Italy last night?"

"This morning, at a ridiculous hour," he said. "I was due for a visit anyway. Don't like being so far from Dad. However, life can be complicated at times." He gazed out of the window for a moment.

"Yes, it certainly can." The extraordinary events that had brought her here flashed through her mind.

"View's incredible isn't it? Well, a bit foggy today but usually."

Indigo nodded, glancing out at the tall trees swaying in the wind. Rain pelted the house. Bedraggled roses stood in shabby rows collecting pools of water in their colourful petals. Finn fiddled with his iPod, pressing it onto the docking station. Elgar's Enigma Variations flowed through the snug kitchen, absorbing the odour of frying deli rashers.

"Do you like classical?"

"Yes, and rock." Indigo took a gulp of tea, wincing in pain as it burned the length of her oesophagus. Finn seemed oblivious to her discomfort.

"Sometimes, when you're surrounded by strong characters you have to distance yourself in order to reach full potential."

Finn turned the rashers with a fork. "Dad and William are great but they're like peas in a pod. I love them but I'm different. Their way is not necessarily mine. Do you like a runny yolk or well done?"

"Cooked but runny." Indigo sipped her tea. "You like cooking?"

"Yes, cooking, art, painting, music... anything creative, I guess."

They sat eating breakfast.

"Do you have a wife or girlfriend in Italy, Finn?"

"No." He mopped up his egg yolk with a piece of French bread. "I live with monks. Not in the wholly religious sense, if you'll pardon the pun. Although I appreciate and follow some of their doctrines... I need the peace and calm they offer and the setting is quite beautiful. The monastery is set up high on the cliffs overlooking the lake."

"Wow, sounds gorgeous! Are you in training?" Indigo was intrigued.

Finn cleared their empty plates. Loading the dishwasher, he shook his head.

"I don't live like a monk, Indigo... must be joking. It's a long and complicated story. I'll bore you with it another time, no doubt." He looked down at her as he took her dirty plate. Inserting a dishwasher tablet into the slot he kicked the door shut. "I did have a long term relationship but it didn't work out. It... proved disappointing in the end." He winced, rubbing the side of his head. "Ahhh...."

"Are you okay?"

"Yes. Sharp pain in the side of my head. I suffer from them sometimes... nothing to worry about, just congestion." Clutching his skull he groaned stamping his foot several times.

A feeling of foreboding filled Indigo. She felt queasy. Two fried eggs on top of a hangover had been a bad idea. Finn's change in behaviour was peculiar too. Perhaps he was having a seizure.

"Can I help? Get you anything?" Anxiety filled her.

"Be okay in a minute!" His face was contorted with pain. Then suddenly his features relaxed and he shook his head.

Indigo stared at him, sensing that under the cheerful and handsome exterior fear, sadness and confusion festered. He hid it well. There was a fleeting look in his eyes too, a faraway searching expression as if he were disconnected from his immediate reality at times. It had appeared several times in the last hour. He was a complex character. She wished William was there to talk to. Suddenly she felt an aching need for physical contact, to feel the security of arms surrounding her, holding her tight. Her spiritual transition was in its infancy. It was a time to take care and be aware of her vulnerability. Negative forces could be camouflaged in many guises.

"There, I'm good. Sorry. You must think me very strange. Just a kinda neuralgia, that's all. I know the weather's vile but do you fancy a ridiculously long walk to a pub somewhere for a few drinks, maybe a bar snack and then stagger back... unless you've got anything else planned?" He gave her a wicked grin. "I'm quite safe, really, contrary to my odd behaviour."

"Yeah, okay. Could do with some fresh air and exercise. Give me half an hour to get showered and ready." Indigo bounded up the stairs. Entering her room she discovered a text message from William.

'Sorry. Make it up to you. Work - sick cover. Wallace's son Finn's here. I'll tell you about him later. He can be odd. Be careful. See you this eve. Wx'

Indigo smiled. Although lunchtime drinking was not part of her new regime it was nice to have the company of another adult and Finn seemed easy to spend time with despite the oddities. After showering she felt better. Dressing in black leggings, white t-shirt with a pink zip-up hoody, she packed her small pink backpack with bottled water, a waterproof jacket, `phone, money and make-up.

Finn was waiting in the hallway. Indigo pulled on her green wellingtons.

"Dad's fed up with being bedridden. The doctor's been and said he can get up tomorrow."

"Should I check on him too? I said to William I would."

"Nah, he's dozing. Had his dinner and left him with a flask of tea and the football. He's happy. We men are simple creatures. Food, drink, sport, music, peace at times and you know the other."

"Cars or motor bikes?"

Finn chuckled.

"You're going to be trouble!" He leaned forward and for a moment Indigo thought he was going to kiss her. Instead he extracted a fleck of fluff from her hair. He seemed oblivious to the usual unspoken space boundaries. Indigo felt awkward as he took her hand, though he seemed to think it was a natural thing to do. His hand was large and warm as it enveloped hers.

"Shall we go on bikes instead? Its light rain now and it'll be quicker."

"Yeah, okay. I've been using your Mum's bike. Wallace said it'd be okay."

"Sure, not like she's going to use it. She gets her exercise in other ways," Finn added scathingly.

Indigo smiled.

"Just need to get my bike out of the studio. Have you been in there?"

"No, but I know about it." Indigo was curious to see the interior of the studio. It could be an ideal place to run her Reiki practice from in the future.

"We converted it so I would have somewhere to paint. It's pretty cool." He led her out of the back door, down a path and through a small white gate to a mud track framed on either side by dark green conifers. Indigo followed him into a dark wood packed full of thin white trees with swaying tops, birds' nests balanced precariously on their outstretched arms. Birdsong and the patter of rain on fallen leaves drowned out the sound of their footsteps. As they rounded a corner, a large old building appeared. Finn extracted a chunky brass key from the back pocket of his jeans and inserted it into the lock of the oak front door.

"Welcome to my world." He waved her in. The old Georgian outbuilding had been tastefully converted into a self-contained studio. Although the main structure was comprised of original bricks, a massive picture window had been inserted. It dominated the far wall, displaying an impressive view of the ocean and jagged cliffs of the east coast of Scotland. The ceiling was high and pitched with whitewashed structural beams. Skylights had been placed at intervals and much of the roof consisted of glass. Turkish rugs lay upon gleaming floorboards and a large inglenook fireplace with a rusty grate stood proudly at the end of the room. A fifty-inch flat screen TV hung from the wall and a comfortable, cream corner sofa wrapped in red rustic throws crouched near the fireplace. An easel with paints was folded neatly in the corner with a stack of canvases.

The back wall was covered by a gigantic oil canvas, the brush strokes perfect, precise and commanding. It was a portrait of a beautiful mermaid sitting on the Bass Rock. Her tail was hidden in the vast waves, but her athletic body had been painted to reveal the splendour of muscle tone and ample breasts. Her face was strong and striking with flawless pale skin, bright green emerald eyes and a small pouting red mouth. Her nose was small and her wavy dark hair hung down her back interwoven with dark green seaweed. In the background the grey sea writhed, attempting to prise her from the safety of her haven back into the icy dark depths. The painting was powerful and thought-provoking. Indigo stood transfixed. She wanted to ask Finn questions about it - the inspiration behind it, who the model was and if she could see some of his other work. The mermaid looked familiar. Finn, however, seemed irritated by her interest in the painting. He pointed to a door.

"This leads to the kitchen, bathroom and bedroom. I see you like the portrait. A local girl... silly idea, really. It's hard to find quality models who will undress. Perhaps you'll pose for me. I need a nude and you'd be perfect for it." His look stripped the clothes from her body and Indigo felt a surge of heat flood to her face.

"I'll pose for you..." William's voice came from the doorway as he walked into the studio. "Been a while since I was last in here, Finn." His tone was full of insinuation. They spun around.

"Whoops, sorry officer..." Finn laughed deeply. "Perfect as you are William, you're the wrong gender and I'm after a different look this time..." He frowned. "I mean..." He glanced up at the mermaid and back to William. "Yes, must have been a while since you've been here." He looked innocently at William, but his eyes were full of confusion. He rubbed his temple with his forefinger.

Indigo felt guilty and embarrassed as if she'd been caught doing something wrong. The atmosphere between William and Finn was full of tension and emotion. William's eyes pierced into Finn's.

"Always suspicious, Will, trying to find answers," Finn said quietly. "You think you can read my mind with those eyes of yours..." He stepped back, seeming hypnotised by William, unable to drop his gaze.

Indigo looked from one to the other. What on Earth was going on? As she watched the two men, William seemed to grow in height and Finn shrink. There was history between them, that was obvious. William seemed to have the upper hand. Perhaps Finn was gay? Maybe he was in love with William? Unrequited love was both cruel and souring, Indigo knew. She had experienced it with Mike. William narrowed his eyes for a moment and then smiled at Finn, removing his cap. His eyes flashed for a second at Indigo.

"You had to work William?" she said obviously, trying to defuse the tension.

"Aye, as bloody usual." He yawned. "Just popped in on my lunch break to check on the old man."

"We're off for a bike ride," said Finn.

"Well at least you'll get some use out of the bike." William stared at Indigo intensely. She looked back at him attempting to read his mood. He seemed annoyed. She'd never known him to be so spikey. "Get us a coffee, Finn," said William, patting him on the shoulder affectionately. The tension evaporated.

"Yeah, sure Will." Finn suddenly embraced William. "Indigo, would you like one?"

"White, one sugar please. Thanks, Finn."

Finn disappeared into the kitchen and Indigo's eyes returned to William's. Standing in front of her, he smoothed a long strand of brown hair back from her face.

"People aren't always who they seem... you know that. Finn's had a few problems... he can be difficult at times... just be aware. Sorry, I'm cranky as hell today. Bit of a hangover and woke up with a crick neck." He lowered his tone to a murmur. "Plus, I wanted to spend the day with you." Indigo was surprised by his words. He had never been so open. The previous evening spent together talking had built trust and made a difference. Sexual tension sizzled between them and Indigo felt an overwhelming urge to touch his chest. He was so close to her. Too near.

"You should have used one of the beds," she said carefully, trying to keep her voice even.

"Yes, I should, shouldn't I?"

He smiled into her eyes. For a moment they just stared at each other. He leaned forward and brushed his lips softly against hers. Wrapping his arms around her, he kissed her harder. She could feel his hard chest muscles pressing against her body. Opening her mouth she kissed him back, gasping at the intensity of the sensations flooding through her. His hands caressed her, trailing up over her breasts. Indigo arched her body into his; her breathing was heavy and she felt almost drugged. With effort he pushed her from him. Holding her head in his hands, his eyes were full of light.

"I've wanted to do that ever since I first saw you. That night you screamed your head off like a lunatic in the campervan," he whispered. Taking a moment to regain his composure, he let go and stood looking at her. "Indigo..."

"Yes?"

"Be patient... please... things are difficult." He ran his fingers down her face lightly. She nodded as he walked to the door. "Tell Finn sorry I've had to go back to work. I'll catch up with him later." He left abruptly, leaving Indigo staring at the empty doorway in bewilderment.

How odd everything seemed all of a sudden. What did William mean when he said that people weren't what they seemed? He echoed the warning of the old Egyptian. Was he referring to himself or Finn, and what did he mean by things being difficult? Indigo wished he would just say what he meant. He obviously felt that he couldn't talk freely with Finn in the kitchen. There was definitely something weird going on between the two of them.

Walking into the kitchen to cancel the coffee, she saw Finn standing by the kettle staring into space. He jumped as she entered.

"Kettle's taking for ever," he said vaguely.

"Helps if you plug it in." Indigo picked up the white lead. "You okay? William's had to go."

Finn seemed a bit disturbed. He turned to Indigo with trembling lips, his eyes watery with suppressed emotion. "It's being back here... and seeing William!" Sadness surrounded him. She nodded. Trickles of water spilled from his eyes. Indigo rubbed his back like she did with the children when they were upset.

"It'll be okay," she muttered reassuringly. Finn wiped his eyes with the palm of his hand.

"Just overwhelmed. Been away a while."

"Why does it upset you seeing William? Is it because you've missed him?"

Finn shrugged awkwardly.

"Yes and no... it's his eyes..." He took a deep breath. "My long-term partner was his cousin, Ella. She's two years older than us and they have similar eyes... looks... Every time I look at him, I see her." He put his head in his hands for a moment. "Just threw me. I thought about this before I boarded the `plane. I was sure I'd be okay."

"It's all right." Indigo patted him on the arm. "How long ago did you split up?"

Finn's blue eyes glazed over for a moment, beads of sweat forming on his forehead. Shaking his head he went to the sink and poured a glass of water. Indigo could feel her stomach churning. Her pulse began to race and blackness threatened to encompass her. She was tuning into Finn's turmoil, to his dark despair. In the kitchen earlier she had felt desperate for affection and physical closeness but it was clear now that these were his needs, not hers. For some reason she was experiencing his emotions. Taking a deep breath, she joined him at the sink and shared his water. Silently she asked the angels to protect her and her aura from all negative outside forces and imagined a shimmering force field of white surrounding her. Her head cleared. Finn also seemed to recover.

"She died." He said quietly, looking down at the red stone floor tiles. An icy shiver shot through Indigo and she reeled back in horror. Finn leaned his head onto her shoulder and sobbed silently. "It was a while ago now, years I think, but it still hurts like hell." He grimaced and blew his nose noisily into a black silk handkerchief. "I miss her so much!" He ran his fingers through his blond hair. "Let's not talk about it anymore. You must think I'm a complete nutter! Dunno about you but I'm dying for a drink."

◆ ◆ ◆

The rain was now hammering onto the glass skylights, banging and pinging. Finn found some bright orange fluorescent water-proof trousers in an old trunk and they giggled as they put them on, adding jackets. Moments later, clad in the waterproofs, they cycled at speed in the pouring rain down narrow country lanes lined with dark green trees and weaving through yellow wheat and pasture fields towards the Auld Inn in the next village.

"Race ya!" yelled Finn.

Speeding down the lane, they dodged large, deep puddles that lay at intervals. The fresh, cold air was exhilarating. As water saturated her face, Indigo was glad that she'd brought her make-up bag with her. They arrived neck and neck at the inn and stood in the doorway, stripping off the wet waterproofs and hanging them on pegs to dry.

"Nearly beat you," said Indigo.

"No chance!" Finn grinned. "You're not the only one who's competitive!"

Despite it being September, fires had been lit for the air was cold and damp. A stocked bar lined the walls and the smell of home cooking greeted them. Squashy leather sofas resting upon varnished oak flooring surrounded a wood-burning stove, inviting them to rest. A few locals drinking pints of lager were seated at the bar. Finn headed to the red gleaming bar to order drinks while Indigo fled to the Ladies bathroom.

The room was ornate with huge mirrors, modern cream fittings and a strong odour of apple liquid soap. Pools of mascara lay beneath her eyes. She looked like one of the pandas at Edinburgh Zoo. Redoing her face, she leaned on the sink and breathed deeply, taking a moment to reflect on the kiss from William. It had taken all his willpower to let her go. The chemistry between them was powerful and magnetic. The kiss had been soft, strong and sensual. Then there was Finn's revelation. It made her realise how little she knew William. In fact she had probably discovered more about Finn in the few hours she had known him than she had about William in weeks.

So, William had lost his cousin and Finn his partner. Indigo wondered what had happened. Finn seemed on the edge, absolutely brimming with unresolved issues and emotion. The need to talk bubbled away within him. She imagined that Wallace and William were not the type of men to have a heart-to-heart, not with another man anyway. She wondered too what his life with the monks was like. No wonder he'd run to Italy to seek solace within the peaceful spirituality offered by monastic life. Although Finn was clearly unstable, she felt drawn to him. And despite William's warning she felt safe in his company. The Egyptian's dark eyes flashed through her mind and she scowled at the reminder.

Cycling had brought colour to her naturally pale face and her skin held a healthy glow. Her eyes were dark blue, bright and huge in her face. Her long dark hair hung in damp tresses down her back. Returning to the pub, she found Finn sitting on a brown leather sofa by the fire. A bottle of red wine and glasses sat on the table alongside a carafe of mineral water.

"I quite liked the panda look." He chuckled at her outraged expression. "You're a beautiful woman, Indigo. No wonder William's got the hots for you." He patted the sofa next to him. A red blush came over her face.

"He's just being friendly," she muttered awkwardly.

"Yes, guys are great at being 'just friends' with attractive women..."

Indigo sat down next to him.

"It's nice to meet you, Finn. Are you staying a while, do you think?"

"Not sure." He took a sip of wine. "I need my life with the monks but it's both beneficial and damaging at the same time. It's not too healthy to be shut off from everyday life. Easy to go into yourself, but less easy to come out again." Indigo nodded. "I'm an artist. I get completely absorbed in my work. Then I talk and pray with the monks and live a life removed from society. My reality is confused at the best of times. Not sure the isolation is helping."

"How d'you mean?"

Finn drained his glass and Indigo took a gulp of her wine.

"For example, if I'm working on a painting, say, a landscape full of vivid colours, and then I go for a walk, I think I'm walking inside my painting - that the landscape I'm walking in is my own creation. I don't mean I think I'm God who created the Earth. I mean, I don't know what's real and what's imaginary... sometimes the two merge. Indigo, I have no concept of time. I don't mean like what time it is today," - he glanced at his watch - "obviously it's two-thirty. I mean with regard to events that have occurred. I haven't a clue when I last saw William. He knows. I pretend I know, but I don't. I spend so much time living in my subconscious. I couldn't tell you when Ella died or any of the facts. I just know that she left me and is no longer here..." His voice trailed off. "I expect you think I'm mental!"

"No, I don't. I think you've had a tough time. Have you had any counselling?"

Finn shook his head and clenched his hands together. "Only by the monks."

"Was it your idea to go to Italy?"

Finn's brow puckered. He shrugged, rubbing his finger in an agitated manner up and down his temple.

"I guess. To be honest, I can't remember. It's all a bit fuzzy."

"Have you heard of 'defence mechanisms', Finn?"

"With relation to what?"

"Sometimes if a person experiences something painful or a series of difficult events in their life, then their defence mechanisms kick in. Sometimes it can be overactive, though. Basically, if the conscious can't cope with what has happened the subconscious takes over and shuts the traumatic event away in the recesses of the mind. Then you get emotional numbness. When the subconscious thinks you can cope again, it begins to leak the reality of the situation back into the conscious mind. So maybe that's why you have blanks - times when you can't remember things."

"You think that's why I don't know what happened to Ella, or when I last saw William, 'cause it's too much for me to deal with? Sounds bizarre."

"A possibility. Either that or you have something else going on."

"You're not a shrink are you?"

"Almost."

"What does that mean?"

"I dropped out of my training... was years ago. I married young while still at university and had a few problems with my husband..." Indigo gave an involuntary shudder, "...couldn't cope with the work load on top of everything else. And yes, I do regret it. I should have dealt with things differently but I didn't. We live and learn, if you pardon the cliché."

"True." He fiddled with his glass. "Have you considered going back to it now?"

"No, that sort of training takes years and I'm too old and too broke."

"What made you decide to come up here, then?"

Indigo took a sip of wine, absentmindedly wiping lipstick

from the rim of the glass with her thumb. "Well, it was a few factors really. My kids are almost grown up. They're both at university. Things got a bit much in Kent. Work was stressful... boss was a pig, always picking away at me," she took a deep breath, "and the guy I'd been seeing – Mike - turned out to be a monster. I was exhausted."

"Violent?"

Indigo nodded, aware that Finn was good at extracting information. She would have to be careful. "A bit, yes."

"I don't understand men who are like that." Finn winced again, rubbing his temple. "Excuse me." He took out a menthol inhaler. "You're so delicate, Indigo - small, slim and fragile-looking. Was it bad?"

"So so, it could have been worse. It was the put-downs and mind games that really did the damage. Then I discovered Reiki - have you heard of it?"

"Yes, I've had it before. Thought it was amazing. Only had two sessions though, wish I'd carried on with it."

Indigo nodded. "Reiki completely transformed my life. My mind cleared and I felt much more energetic. I came up here for a weekend in the campervan and met William, who introduced me to Wallace - and here I am."

"When you say your mind cleared, what do you mean?"

Indigo drained her glass. Finn was interested in her experience and was naturally homing in on the parts that were relevant to him.

"For the last ten years my mind's been foggy. It was as if my head was stuffed full of a thick substance pressing down on my brain, hampering my ability to think clearly. My blood pressure's slightly low and I thought that was the cause. But after my first session of Reiki, my mind cleared. It was amazing. Suddenly everything began to make sense again. Clarity returned. Everything seemed magnified - sight, sound, even my sense of smell. It was such a relief. Prior to Reiki I was completely lacking in energy."

Finn refilled their glasses and opened bags of salted peanuts. "Carry on."

"When I was young I always listened to my intuition, gut instinct if you like. It was second nature. But after a number of bad experiences, especially with men, I began to question it. I couldn't understand why it was so inaccurate. For example, I'd meet someone new, say a guy, and think he was really nice and genuine and then he'd turn out not to be. When I met Mike, my last partner, I thought 'Wow, what a great guy' but he turned out to be selfish, aggressive and treated me like shit. Lately, I've been thinking about my first impression of him and how I felt. Truly felt." Indigo took a slug of wine. "Am I boring you?"

"No. No, carry on." Finn emptied half a bag of peanuts into his mouth.

"I thought Mike was great because I wanted him to be. I wanted a cosy, stable relationship with a man who knew what he was doing with his life. I was attracted to him physically. There was sexual chemistry. I liked the fact that he was wealthy and successful, not because I'm a gold digger but because he had energy, drive and direction. But in truth my intuition set off warning bells at our first meeting - and again later. There were many times when I thought of him and felt that unwelcome, fleeting, dull sensation in my stomach or solar plexus or an uncomfortable nagging feeling, or emptiness... But my ego overruled those feelings because I was determined to have the relationship I wanted with him."

"So you had a feeling it was wrong but ignored it because you wanted the relationship to work." Finn nodded. "Hmm... think I've done that before."

"I extracted the positive aspects of Mike and put them together in my mind, creating the character I wanted. I clung to the character my ego created despite his actions and words. The ego is good at justifying negative things in order to preserve something that we hold dear. That's what I think anyway." She took a swig of wine.

"I think I get what you're saying."

"It's probably obvious to a lot of people but it wasn't obvious to me. When we first meet someone they're always on their best behaviour because they want you to like them. After a while their true self leaks through. If they're a bad character in reality, like Mike, then it's devastating to see it. Furthermore, when they begin to be themselves, we tend to blame ourselves for the way they treat us. Thinking it's a flaw in our character that has brought out the worst in theirs. We make excuses for them – they're stressed out at work or finding adjusting to a relationship difficult. We hang on to our first impression and idea of them because we're desperate to believe that they are the person we first thought. But, we'll never get that person back because they don't exist. It was just their public image."

"You are so right!" Finn nodded again, leaning forward.

"If you take the ego away and the justifications and see the cold facts and couple that with your first intuition of that person... then you have a clear picture. That's the time to walk away. If I'd done that with Mike it would have saved a great deal of heartache and misery. On the other hand, it may not have brought me here. Also, I've strengthened as a person, I've discovered Reiki and as a result I've had many positive experiences." Indigo picked up her wine glass and took a sip. "Sorry, I'm rambling."

"Not at all... funny how life works. Even a bad experience can lead to good ones. I think you'd have made a good shrink, by the way."

Indigo took a handful of peanuts. "Bad can only lead to good if you make some positive conscious choices and put them into action. Tell me about your paintings. You're art is excellent. Well, what I've seen of it."

Finn smiled. "Painting is my life."

He ordered another bottle of wine and they spent the afternoon chatting idly about art, Reiki and travel. About five o'clock they cycled back to the studio, weaving about the quiet country lane singing old rock songs at the tops of their voices. Finn lit a fire in the inglenook and began dragging out blank canvases and assembling his easel. Indigo lay on the sofa covered by a rug; she must have drifted off to sleep because when she awoke it was night-time. The heat from the fire pressed on her face as the logs spat and hissed in the grate. The room was lit by a tall lamp in the far corner. She could hear raised voices. Sitting up on her elbow she saw Finn and William standing over by the easel. Finn had his shirt sleeves rolled up. Smears of yellow and purple paint covered his muscular lower arms. William looked cross.

"We only went for a drink, William," Finn slurred slightly, his body swaying. He'd obviously carried on drinking.

"She's been through a lot. She doesn't need you corrupting her!"

"What's that supposed to mean?" Finn reached down and took a slug out of the wine bottle by his side.

"I think you know! I'm taking her home. I had hoped that your time with the monks had helped."

"It has - did. Okay! PC Sanctimonious Macleod." He hiccupped loudly and grinned. "Okay." He gave a theatrical sweep with his arm, gesturing from the sofa to the door, splattering red wine over the floor. "Take her home to your bed. She's a pal, that's all." He staggered backwards slightly. William shook his head in exasperation. Indigo lay her head back down on the maroon cushion pretending to be asleep. She could hear William's footsteps coming towards her. Opening her eyes, she saw him crouch down in front of her.

Shaking her gently, he whispered, "Indigo. You've fallen asleep at Finn's. I'm gonna take you home." He lifted her carefully. "See you later, Finn," he said.

"Sure you don't wanna stay for a drink?"

"Not tonight."

Indigo could feel the cold air on her face as they went outside. It had finally stopped raining.

"I can walk William."

"You're a bit worse for wear. You can pick your bike up tomorrow. An early night for you, I think." Entering the house he removed her Wellingtons and carried her up the stairs to her room. Placing her in bed, he covered her over. "I'll fetch you a hot chocolate." He stroked her face. "The weather forecast is good for the end of the month. I thought we could all go for a swim in the loch. It'll be too cold soon."

Indigo shut her eyes. She felt comfortably drunk. William must be insane, she mused. The loch would be about minus two already. He probably thought it was suitable for swimming because it hadn't yet iced over. She could hear the soft murmur of William's voice and the sound of the wind howling around the building and the waves crashing on the seashore. The bed covers felt warm and comforting. She reached out and took his hand.

"I'm still in transition, still finding my way," she muttered. Her eyelids closed and sleep engulfed her.

TWO

Suspicion

Indigo awoke the next day with a renewed determination to follow the spiritual path. This would involve daily Reiki, exercise, meditation and less alcohol. She would stay positive despite the daily challenges, and overcome the past. It was time to move forward. The behaviour and thought patterns of the last forty years would take time to alter but as her energy shifted to a higher vibration she would become more positive and energetic. It was imperative that she start applying spirituality to her daily life.

Her children Charlie and Lily arrived later that day for a two week visit before returning to university. The weather was cold but bright and sunny so they wrapped up in hats, gloves and thick jackets before venturing out to the city. Keen to explore Edinburgh, they climbed the lush green rocky trail to the top of Arthur's Seat. The air was clear and the views spectacular. Edinburgh Castle, an imposing cluster of historical architecture, teetered on the hilltop opposite dominating the skyline. Glittering coastline stretched out for miles.

The remaining days were spent enthralled by Phantom of the Opera at Edinburgh Playhouse, sampling a variety of dishes at city restaurants and creeping through the sinister, dark and musty Edinburgh Dungeons. After exploring the capital they wandered along the coastal paths of East Lothian, lunching at inns scattered nearby. By the time the children returned to university, Indigo felt positive and happy. Lily and Charlie had remarked on how much brighter and younger she appeared and confided how relieved they'd been when she left Mike. Wallace joined them for dinner on a number of occasions but William was busy working and Finn shut himself away in his studio to paint.

Two days after the children left, Indigo received a text from William asking if she would like to go swimming in the loch the next day. He'd also asked Finn. If they wanted to, he'd collect them at eleven. Indigo looked out of the window at the grey, rain-soaked day and smiled. She texted back that she'd love to go for a swim.

The next morning, a column of white sunlight glistened through a gap in the bedroom curtains. The light azure sky was clear. The sea sparkled slate blue with huge, frothy white breakers giving an illusion of warmth. Indigo dressed in layers of clothing in preparation for the cold. William arrived promptly at eleven in the same white van he used for gardening jobs. Indigo slid into the front seat while Finn clambered into the back of the van. A clanging and clattering followed as he cleared a space amidst the shovels, dried dirt and various garden tools. William leaned over and kissed Indigo on the cheek. His lips felt soft and she could smell his aftershave, a tangy musky scent. Heat rushed to her face.

"I've missed you," he whispered.

Indigo smiled into his eyes for a moment before looking down at her hands. She wasn't used to the open and warm version of William yet. He surprised her.

"It's been a while," she murmured awkwardly, suddenly feeling shy.

"Too long. But you had a nice time with your kids?"

"Yes, great. We did the sightseeing tour. Castle, dungeons, shopping, that sort of thing. They look so grown up. Well, I guess they are."

William smiled.

"Aye. They don't stay bairns for long, that's for sure."

Entering William's parents' small estate, the van bumped over a series of deep potholes. There was a crash as Finn toppled over.

"Will! You bugger! You did that on purpose!" Finn yelled from the back of the van.

William chuckled to himself. All previous tension between them seemed to have dispersed. Finn was in good spirits. Maybe painting solidly for two weeks had done him good.

"I've built a fire and brought some supplies," said William.

Parking the van near the loch, William unloaded an indignant and moaning Finn from the back of the van.

"Had a shovel right up my backside. You could've cleared out the van, Will!" Finn made a fuss of brushing mud off his black jeans.

Lighting the bonfire, William placed a picnic basket and some rugs with waterproof lining at a safe distance. Trees framing the curve of the loch bent towards the water in greeting. The steely liquid was dark, cold and forbidding. A weak autumn sun beat down happily.

"We'll wait for the fire to catch before swimming. It'll be cold. Sure you're up for it, Finn?" He winked at Indigo. William was wearing jeans, hiking boots and a black sweater. His hair was swept back from his face and his healthy green eyes shone with amusement.

"See that old rope hanging from the tree over there?" Finn pointed to the trees on the far bank of the loch. "That's where we used to play as kids, Will and I. See who could swing out the furthest and dive bomb into the water."

"Sounds fun."

"Yes it was," he said wistfully. "Such a relief after the strict regime of boarding school... We used to run wild in the summer holidays."

The fire popped and hissed as the thick, damp wood above the kindling dried and caught alight. Soon orange flames roared upwards licking the cold air. The two men stripped down to their swimming shorts. William's physique was defined, toned and lean, while Finn was taller, broad and stocky. Both men were healthy and fit. The walking, running and cycling with the children had kept Indigo in good shape too. As she peeled off her chunky sweater and tracksuit to reveal a blue bikini she was pleased that she'd made the effort. Both men gave her body the once over and Indigo cringed with embarrassment. She was about to grab a towel when they turned and plunged into the water. Racing, they reached the far bank head to head.

"Come on, English!" yelled William. "Or do I have to come and fetch you?"

Indigo dipped her toe tentatively into the ice cold water. Why had she worn a skimpy summer bikini? A wet suit would have been more appropriate. She took a deep breath and plunged into the dark coldness. Her first instinct was fear as the icy water knocked the breath out of her but she fought the urge to flee the bitter cold. The two men were standing on the bank waving and shouting encouragement. Indigo didn't want to appear weak or inferior, so she pushed herself forward and swam with all her strength. As she reached the other side William wrapped his arms around her rubbing away the cold with his hands as her body shook and teeth rattled.

"You two are mental!" she gasped. "It's Baltic!"

"We're gonna dive bomb into the water from the rope," Finn said, pointing to the weathered and discoloured rope hanging from the tree. "You first because you're frozen and need to get to the warm fire, then me because I'm younger than William," he grinned.

Pulling back the rope, Indigo ran at the loch. As she reached maximum height and length she dropped, curled into a ball. For a moment a frozen silence encased her as her whole body submerged. Rising to the surface, she swam strongly to the shore. The sight of the warm blazing fire urged her on. Brain-freeze threatened as she grabbed her thick, cream bath sheet and wrapped her body in one of the rugs. She soaked up the warmth provided by the flames and rubbed her ears.

Finn reached the fire next. He dried himself and dressed rapidly.

"Brrr... bloody hell, that was freezing. You did really well!" His blue eyes twinkled at Indigo. "Damn cold! Bit different to Lake Garda."

"Bet it is. Do you swim there?"

"Crack of dawn, most days."

Finn picked up the mobile `phone buzzing on top of a pile of discarded clothes.

"William's `phone. Will!" he called.

William had gone for a longer swim and was at the other end of the loch. Indigo pulled on her tracksuit and jumper, idly watching Finn. The buzzing stopped and then started again.

"Might be work," Finn muttered and answered the call, imitating William's broader accent. "PC MacLeod." The colour drained from his face. Gasping, his body began to shake. He slumped to the ground and pressed 'End call'.

"What's the matter?" demanded Indigo. "Finn, what is it?"

"Nothing..." he whispered.

"Was it bad news? Who was it?"

"No-one. Wrong number," Finn said vaguely. His eyes were glassy and unfocused.

Puzzled, Indigo took in his reaction. He appeared to be in shock. The fire popped and hissed, casting orange sparks out onto the rug. Finn shook his head as if suddenly aware of his surroundings. Looking down at the `phone he punched the touch screen and Indigo heard Finn's `phone bleep.

"I think I left the gas hob on in the kitchen," he said in a strange, strangled voice. "I've got weeks of work, valuable paintings there. I'll jog back." He glared at Williams' swimming form cutting through the ink. "See you later," he said absently, and began to jog back past the van.

"Finn, I can drop you back!" Indigo called. What was the matter with him?

Turning, he bellowed at her.

"NO!" His face was a mask of dark rage. His blue twinkly eyes were as black as the waters of the loch. "Leave me!" He raced away at speed in the direction of home.

Indigo stared at the angry figure for a moment before picking up William's discarded `phone. She pressed the display for the last number. 'Alle'. So it was a regular contact. Alle would be in his address book. She looked at the list of sent text messages. Finn had sent himself Alle's contact details. Why? He'd been too shocked by 'something' not to bother covering his tracks. Indigo could see William swimming back to shore so she quickly replaced the `phone. Something weird was going on.

William clambered out of the water.

"Where's Finn?" he asked, grabbing an enormous black towel.

"Gone home, I think. He was okay one minute and then he turned really weird... said he thought he'd left the gas on."

"He does that."

William towelled himself dry, dressing in warm clothes. Opening a flask, he poured two cups of steaming hot chocolate then pulled out a frying pan and a small gas camping stove. For some reason, Indigo felt reluctant to tell William about the missed call and how it had altered Finn's mood. They so rarely spent time together alone and William seemed happy and relaxed. The news of the call would change that.

"Got some quorn sausages especially for you," William smiled. His long dark lashes were stuck together and his green eyes were almost luminous after the exhilaration of the swim. "You okay? Don't worry about Finn, Indigo. He's moody at the best of times. Probably time he returned to the monks. He finds normal life difficult. We'll not let him spoil our morning. I've only got until two o'clock then I've got to go into work."

"You work a lot," Indigo commented, watching sausages sizzling in the pan and slowly turning brown.

The aroma of the hot sausages mingled with that of burning wood. Indigo's stomach rumbled loudly as she sipped her hot chocolate. It tasted rich and delicious, spreading heat throughout her insides.

"One of the guys at the station caught chickenpox from his two year old. Completely wiped him out - apparently it's worse when you're older. So I'm covering some of his shifts until we get someone from another station. Budget cuts don't make cover easy."

Contented, they sat side by side eating sausage sandwiches and drinking hot chocolate, enjoying the warmth provided by the orange and purple flames. The squawking of seagulls in the breeze intermittently broke the silence.

"I live in a cabin through the trees." William pointed away from the main house to the far end of the loch.

Indigo was surprised as she had presumed wrongly that he still lived with his parents. It was such a vast white house.

"Bit old to live with my parents," William smiled, following her thoughts. "They're away in Dubai at present. I keep an eye on the place for them."

"A cabin?"

"Yes. It's like a Swiss chalet. It has all the mod cons. My Dad had it built years ago to rent out to tourists for extra income. It's paid for itself over and over since. People love the surroundings. It's coastal, scenic and tucked away here."

Indigo was about to ask him about Finn and his cousin Ella when William glanced at his watch.

"Damn, time to go. Come and have dinner with me at the cabin one evening? I'm not bad with a tin opener."

"Sure. Love to."

Packing up and dousing the fire, they returned to the van

and drove back to Wallace's. Finn's reaction to the call nagged away at her. William seemed to consider mood swings were the norm for Finn so perhaps the `phone call hadn't been the trigger, although she suspected otherwise. As they approached the house, she blurted out: "You had a missed call."

William glanced at her with raised eyebrows.

"When you were swimming. There was a missed call on your mobile."

"Oh?"

"Finn answered it. That was when he went all strange."

A guarded look slid over William's handsome face. His mouth tightened and his expression turned blank. Parking on the gravel in front of the Georgian house, he grabbed his `phone.

"You didn't think to tell me before?"

"I was going to... didn't know whether to... you were in a good mood and I didn't want to spoil anything..." she trailed off, wriggling with discomfort in her seat. A dull feeling sat at the bottom of her stomach as William tapped the call button.

"Alle." He looked startled. "And you say Finn answered the call?"

"Yes, why?"

"Well, there's no surprise that he reacted the way he did. Shit!"

"What do you mean?"

A fleeting expression swept across his face. Guilt. But why?

"William?"

"The call was from my cousin Ella. They..."

"But she's dead..." interrupted Indigo.

William's glared at her sharply, his eyes darkening defensively. He rubbed his forehead with his fingertips and took in a deep breath.

"Indigo, she's no more dead then you or I." His tone was stern.

"But he told me she was. He said... why would he make it up?" Indigo shook her head in confusion. "I don't understand. William, what the hell's going on? The other day at the studio I could feel the tension between you. This morning you were both fine. Then there's a mysterious missed call from Finn's dead girlfriend to you and now you say Ella's not dead when Finn says she is. Why would he say that?"

"He thinks she is." William leaned his forehead for a moment on the steering wheel. "What a mess. How stupid of me to leave my `phone there. I never thought for a minute. Idiot!"

"Why would Finn think she's dead?" Indigo persisted, her mind racing to previous conversations she'd had with Finn. He'd been extremely vague about Ella's death, saying that he couldn't remember any times or dates. "What about the funeral?"

"Finn's not right, Indigo - in the head. He's okay sometimes. It's a nightmare situation with him, all messed up and complicated. There was no funeral. Ella's not dead, not outside of Finn's head anyway."

Suddenly William looked tired and pale. Indigo could sense the energy draining out of him. His `phone bleeped and he swore. "That's my sergeant. I'm late, got to go. I'll explain everything to you later. Stay away from Finn. I mean it!" William frowned at her. "When he's in this state he can turn nasty."

Indigo frowned in disbelief. Finn might be eccentric and moody but he didn't appear the violent type. An image of his eyes flashing black with rage flashed through her mind. She hadn't thought that Mike was aggressive either to begin with. Her first instinct regarding Finn was that he was a decent person but riddled with pent up emotional anguish and hurt.

"I've really got to go. I'm sorry this has involved you, Indigo. It's not what you need." He kissed her on the cheek. Burying his face in her neck for a moment, he inhaled her scent. "Call you later."

Indigo walked to the house. Picking up the post, she flicked through it. The envelopes were mainly addressed to Wallace with a couple for her that looked like bills. She'd deal with them another day. Suddenly she felt weary. It had been a great morning apart from the trouble caused by the strange call. Wallace's car was absent from its usual spot and she discovered a folded note from him on the table in the hallway. He'd gone to his holiday home in Tenerife for a week or so with a friend. His hip was bothering him and he needed heat and a change of scene.

Indigo selected some meditation music on her iPod and ran a bath. Sinking into the hot and soothing, sensual waters she tried to focus on a creative visualisation of a South Seas island. Concentration proved difficult as her mind was a whirl with the events of the morning and she felt exhausted. She was still in recovery herself. William was right. All this disruption was not what she needed; however it was life. If relationships with human beings were to be formed, there would always be complications and problems. By the age of forty most people had life experiences and emotional issues that affected their present.

Dozing in and out of the visualisation, her eyes closed. The South Seas island had clean, soft white sand. The emerald ocean was calm with gentle lapping waves and a dark cobalt sky untarnished by clouds. Swaying golden palm trees spouting dark green leaves boasted an abundance of bananas and coconuts, offering shade from the sun's powerful rays. Disturbingly, Finn's face and her immediate reality kept interfering with her inner paradise, demanding analysis and answers. Finn must truly believe that Ella was dead. He had appeared upset and she could sense his pain and inner torment. Maybe he was unwell and delusional. Had William and Wallace explained the truth to him? Surely they hadn't told him she was dead? That would be too shocking! The question that also arose was why Ella contacted William in secret, and why did he have her on his 'phone as 'Alle', Ella backwards?

Finn seemed aware of his problems. He had revealed to her that his reality was confused, that he had no concept of time, so it wasn't as if he was in denial about his mental health. Could it be that he had invented her death for some reason? It was all very odd.

Letting out the cold water, she refilled the bath with steaming hot water. She had to distance herself from the situation with William, Finn and Wallace. Although the three men had already become dear to her, it was not her journey. The kiss with William immediately entered her thoughts. If she entered into a romantic partnership with him, then his life would merge with hers. Also, she was lying in Wallace's bathtub and Finn was his son. Whatever was going on did affect her whether she liked it or not. In confirmation, her mobile 'phone began to flash. It was a text from Finn. He wanted to meet urgently. He was at the top of North Berwick Law.

The sky darkened to an iron grey and rain began to lash against the windows. Indigo felt warm and relaxed in the bathtub and for a moment wondered whether she should ignore the text. After all, William had warned her to stay away from Finn when he was in a disturbed state of mind. However, the expression on Finn's face when he had answered the call had been tortured. Reluctantly, she pulled herself from the bath and rapidly dressed in clean, dry clothes. Drying her hair, she applied light make-up before pulling on a large waterproof jacket. The last thing she felt like doing was trekking up North Berwick Law in the wind and rain.

◆ ◆ ◆

The hill watched over the town and surrounding areas. Standing at 613 feet high, it was an enjoyable climb on a fine summer day, boasting spectacular views across East Lothian and to Fife in the distance. Pulling out her bike, she began to cycle along Tantallon Road. By the time she reached the Law she was tired from battling against the elements. She texted Finn and asked where he was, then began to climb the lush green hillside. The route was slippery and despite wearing trainers she fell several times, muddying her jogging bottoms. By the time she'd climbed three-quarters of the way she was gasping for breath and still hadn't received a reply. A thin spiral of smoke trickled from the old animal shelter cut into the hillside just before the summit. Indigo headed towards it.

Finn was sitting on a rug on the concrete floor of the shelter. He had lit a Tilly lamp and built a small fire. Swigging Jack Daniels out of a litre bottle, he grinned weakly at her. Smears of dirt covered his face. It was clear that he'd been crying. Indigo felt a tug of guilt at her reluctance to meet him. He was a tortured soul.

"Sorry to drag you up here, Indigo," he said quietly, "especially in such lousy weather. Used to come here when I's a kid. Whenever I's upset... which was most of the time."

Indigo sat down next to him on the edge of the blanket. The heat from the small fire was welcoming; although she was warm from exertion, her knees felt chilled. Finn offered her a drink and she was about to refuse but took a swig instead. The strong spirit seeped into every aspect of her being, immediately heating her from the inside out. Taking another gulp, she handed the bottle back to Finn.

"Haven't drunk Jack Daniels for years," she commented. "It brings out my wicked alter ego so I banned myself from it."

Finn smiled.

Indigo decided to remain silent. He would talk when he needed to and so they sat there drinking, huddled together and feeding the fire from the pile of sticks.

"I don't understand," Finn murmured pitifully. "I'm terrified, Indigo. Have I lost my mind?" He bit his knuckle as tears coursed down his face. Indigo was unsure what to say. She didn't want to provoke Finn or cause him more distress but he deserved the truth.

"William said that Ella is alive, but you think she's dead."

Finn swung his gaze to hers.

"What d'you mean?" Hope filled his eyes.

"I don't know much. He had to go back to work. He was pretty cut up. Said there was no funeral and the only funeral that existed was the one in your head."

"So I'm a nutcase. Why the hell would I invent something that would rip my heart out?" He sounded angry. "He said... I'm sure... and Dad, they told me she was gone. Gone for good. I can't remember! Why can't I remember?" He punched the side of his head. "Was I drunk, deluded, brainwashed or am I just bloody mental? All my life... I've always been different... odd! Never fitted in at home, nor at school, and now this." He began to sob in despair.

Indigo grabbed his wrist.

"Punching yourself isn't going to find answers, Finn," she said gently. Drawing him into her arms, he cried like a small boy and she wondered if his mother had ever shown him affection and comfort; or had Ruby been too preoccupied with her lovers to bother with her complex gifted son? "You're a lovely man, Finn, and a talented artist. There's nothing wrong with being a bit different to other people."

"No there isn't," he sniffed, wiping his face with his sleeve. "But there is something wrong with everyone making you feel like a freak. I'm not a weak man, Indigo, despite what they say. Yes, I'm emotional but I am strong. I'm just confused. If I have problems, I need to know. If I've been lied to, I need to know. I don't care who said what. I just want the truth."

"Do you remember when we were chatting in the pub the

other day and I said that sometimes defensive mechanisms block memories?"

Finn nodded.

"Well, sometimes, if something awful has happened, then an alternative reality is preferable to facing what actually occurred."

"Yeah, I get that. But what could have been so awful? Why would I have invented her death when I adored her? Why would death have been preferable to her living?"

"What if she'd left you, Finn?"

He winced.

"She would never... she loved me just as much. She would never leave me. Ever!" Rubbing the side of his head, he took a long drink. "We loved each other passionately. Why would she?"

"No idea. Just speculating, trying to discover answers. I don't know any more than you do. The only people with the truth are William and possibly Wallace."

Finn's eyes narrowed.

"Unless..." He ran his fingers through his hair. "Unless William invented a story to get me out of the way. Yes, I bet that's what happened. He shipped me off to bloody Italy under the care of his pal from the army." He glanced at Indigo's increasingly confused expression. "William was in the army years ago. One of his pals was a chaplain. He left the army and became a monk at the monastery at Riva del Garda - hence my stay there. This is insane. He must have wanted Ella for himself, which would explain why he's been in secret contact with her. Also why she's on his `phone as Alle." Finn swore fluently. "I'll rip his heart out with my bare hands."

"Finn, this is pure guesswork! You don't know. It's a bit far-fetched. William is Ella's cousin and he's a policeman," she added irrelevantly. Fear gripped her insides. His paranoid line of thought was bizarre.

"Ex-Special Forces. God knows what he's actually capable of." Finn wiped his face dry with his sleeve.

Indigo felt startled once more by how little she knew about William. Who was she to take his side when she didn't even know who he was? She took the bottle from Finn and began to drink. They sat in silence, swigging from the bottle and staring into the flickering flames.

Where had her faith and purpose gone? Finn was too negative for her to be around. She could feel herself spiralling backwards, all the good work unravelling. Then suddenly a warm calm descended. It didn't matter what William had told her about his life. She knew who he was.

"William cares about you, anyone can see that," she insisted, and the tight fist clenching her guts released a little.

Glancing at her `phone she saw that William had texted her demanding to know where she was. It was seven o'clock in the evening. Darkness had descended onto the hillside but the moon was full, offering dim light. A million stars glanced down at them in amusement. Despite defending William, Indigo didn't text him back. Standing up, she stretched her back as her left buttock cheek numbed. She felt unsteady on her feet, beginning to feel drunk.

"Think I've drunk a bit too much JD," she muttered. A white, round beam bobbed up the hillside. Glancing up at the moon, she twisted her mouth.

"How weird..." she spoke loudly.

"Indigo, is that you?" William's deep voice sounded nearby.

"Aye, PC MacLeod! Finn, William's here. It's a torch. Torchlight, not the moon." Turning, she explained to Finn, who nodded sincerely. "I thought it was the moon, William. Thought it had dropped down from the sky to light the way. But it was still in the sky... so confusing... two moons? Still, other planets have more than one moon." She staggered out to greet him.

"Jesus! How much have you had to drink?" William caught her as she toppled towards him, sitting her down onto a soft clump of grass. "Look at the state of you."

The grass was wet and Indigo could feel the cold damp ground seeping through her thin trousers. Away from the warmth of the fire the temperature had dropped considerably. She began to shiver. Shining his torch into the old animal shelter, William took in the empty bottle of Jack Daniels and the glowing red embers of the fire.

"When you said you were into spirits, I didn't think you were referring to this kind." William glared at Indigo, kicking the bottle disdainfully. "Thought I'd find you in your old haunt, Finn," he added in a gentler tone. "We need to talk. Things have got out of hand and confused. Come on." Taking Finn's hand, he hauled him up. Finn followed William outside. Roughly pulling at William's black jacket, he swung him around to face him, swinging his fist and catching William on the cheekbone.

"That's for destroying my life, you lying bastard!"

As William fell he kicked Finn's legs from under him. Finn landed on the mud next to him, momentarily winded.

"What the hell are you talking about? Finn, you were confused - you couldn't acknowledge what happened!"

"You lied to me about Ella's death to get rid of me, so you could have her for yourself!"

Finn lunged at him and they rolled down the hillside, punching and yelling. Indigo picked up William's torch from where he'd dropped it and ran, slipping and sliding after them. As she shone the torchlight on them she saw Finn kick William off him. William fell backwards, hitting the side of his head on a rock. Indigo screamed but William held up his hand.

"Stay where you are," he roared.

He lay stunned for a moment, watching Finn gingerly sitting up. Blood trickled down his neck. Then he swung himself up onto his feet and pounced on Finn. Flipping him over onto his front, he `cuffed him.

"I ought to arrest you for assaulting a police officer, you lunatic!" he shouted, touching his head. William was clearly having trouble controlling his temper, his eyes blazing with anger. "Jesus, Finn!" Hauling Finn onto his feet, he turned to Indigo. Finn swayed back and forth, his eyes glazed from the effects of alcohol. There was a smear of mud down the side of his face and his blond hair stood on end.

"Are you okay, William? Is your head alright?" Indigo's voice slurred. Her hair hung in saturated dreadlocks about her face, mascara beneath eyes that were huge in a deathly pale face.

"It's just a scratch. You're a bloody disgrace!" He glared at her bedraggled state. "Hold the torch steady so we don't end up breaking our necks, can you? It's as slippery as hell."

Rain began to pelt down accompanied by a howling wind. Indigo took a step forward and slipped over onto her backside.

"Christ!" William shouted. "I should leave the pair of you up here - or better, lock you up for the night in a cell. Yes, maybe I'll do that. Give you both a chance to sober up. You're like a couple of badly behaved kids!"

Indigo began to cry. Their friendship was ruined now for certain.

William pulled her up and marched them both down the hill, locking them into the back of the police car. Indigo felt like a criminal and began to giggle.

"You'll get an explanation of what happened two years ago, Finn," William spoke calmly. "But you need to be in a sober state to hear it. I did not steal Ella from you. For God's sake man, you're my best pal. There was no conspiracy to get rid of you. However, there's a lot that happened that might be difficult for you to take in."

Finn hiccupped. His chin sank to his chest and he rolled over, resting his head onto Indigo's lap. She stroked his hair. William raised his eyes to the heavens. Indigo met his gaze in the rear view mirror and a hint of a smile crossed William's lips.

THREE

Hatred

Opening her eyes Indigo found herself alone in the back of the police car. A cruel chill sneaked into the car, cloaking her with freezing breath penetrating to her bones. Approaching footsteps crunched on the gravel and the car door opened. Indigo could see William's profile in the moonlight. His eyes gleamed. Reaching out, she stroked his face.

"Beautiful William."

He glared at her. He looked tired and grumpy.

"Drunken flattery won't get you out of trouble. Come on. It's your turn. I seem to spend most of my time putting other people to bed these days, and not in the way I'd like to."

"Finn?"

"Taken him to the studio and tucked him up."

"Shouldn't you go to hospital?" Indigo murmured. There was a dark red gash on his hairline.

"Just a flesh wound. Cuts to the head always bleed a lot. It looks worse than it is."

The rain had stopped but the wind careered around the grounds, growling in a sinister fashion. The air was heavy with the smell of sea salt and ice and a wall of grey fog slunk towards them from the direction of the coastal path. Removing their muddy shoes, William carried her upstairs to the bedroom. He insisted on peeling off her wet clothes down to her underwear despite her protests. Indigo felt embarrassed and childlike.

"I've seen you in a bikini. What's the difference?"

"This is underwear!" Indigo could feel red heat rising up her cheeks.

"It covers the same parts." William threw the dirty clothes into the laundry basket. "Come on, into bed. I could do with a whisky. You can have a cup of very strong tea."

He hung up his jacket and disappeared downstairs, returning with a tray of tea and whisky. He'd also cleaned the wound on his head and put a small plaster over the cut. He poured out a large glass of amber liquid and handed Indigo a mug of steaming brown tea.

"Do you feel up to talking or are you too inebriated?"

Indigo pulled a face.

"No! I was a bit tipsy but I feel better now."

William sat on the bed next to her with his feet up, sipping whisky.

"A bit? Honestly, what a pair! I specifically said don't go near Finn."

"He texted me, and he's harmless... with me anyway. He needed someone to talk to. Doesn't seem like he has many people to turn to. I don't mean you..." Indigo trailed off.

"I was worried, Indigo."

"I'm a big girl."

"You are. But I saw the bruises, remember. Sorry to bring it up, but I could have murdered your ex when I saw what he'd done to you." Frowning, his eyes darkened with anger.

"Finn's not Mike." Indigo looked down at her hands in renewed embarrassment.

"No, maybe not. Even so he is capable of disturbed behaviour. How the hell am I gonna explain things to him? Jesus, I don't want to completely unhinge him."

Indigo sat up in bed, pulling on her dressing gown.

"Run it past me and I'll tell you what I think - if he'll be able to handle it or not." She smiled. "I'm sorry, William, for acting like a mad lush. I was just trying to be helpful."

"By being Finn's drinking partner?" William grinned. "Yes, you were helpful ironically. He seems to connect to you in a way he rarely does with anyone." He refilled his glass. "I've taken the day off tomorrow. Need to sort him out. Things haven't been easy for you, Indigo, I understand that. So don't be too hard on yourself."

"I had cut down drinking, you know. Just had a blip tonight."

William smiled.

"We all have those, believe me. When I found out the extent of my wife's promiscuity, I went on a bender for months and fell out with everyone in the process."

Indigo nodded.

"Yes, things can spiral out of control. Negative thoughts attract more of their kind until your whole life sucks. Tell me about Finn?"

William took a large swig of his drink.

"When Finn began seeing Ella everything was great. But after about six months he sold a collection of paintings to a gallery owner who ripped him off, leaving him in a whole heap of debt. The sale had been agreed on a verbal basis. There was nothing in writing, no written contract. It was a gentleman's agreement. Unfortunately there was only one gentleman present. The buyer was a low life.

"Finn took it badly. His art work is personal to him. He didn't want the gallery owner to have it, said he was a cheat and not worthy. He went to the gallery one night and broke in and stole his paintings back. Subsequently he was arrested. Ella was furious with him for being naïve and stupid. The paintings were worth thousands and he didn't get a fraction of their value. The police dropped the charges as a 'gentleman's club' favour to Wallace, but after that things started going downhill."

"In what way?"

"Well, lack of money never brings joy, as you know. Ella had moved into the studio with Finn by this time. After modelling for him - the mermaid portrait on the wall - she started modelling for others."

"Ah yes, of course." Indigo could immediately see the resemblance between Ella and William. Finn was right, their eyes and looks were similar.

"Finn forbade her to do nudes or topless." William ran his fingers through his hair. "But Ella's temperamental. Even as a child, if someone told her not to do something then she would do the opposite. She told him she was doing just that, almost porn. She was away working overnight sometimes and Finn was demented with grief. He just couldn't deal with it. The business with the paintings really hurt him. He's really hypersensitive, always has been. He had a terrible time at school and Ruby wasn't exactly Mother Earth. Wallace is ex-Navy. We're all a bit stiff upper lip. Just not what Finn needed... guess he had no-one to relate to. Suddenly he lost his faith in people. Even the woman he loved had gone against him."

"Poor Finn. No wonder he was desperate for love and affection."

"Aye. Pity you weren't around then. But then he went really weird. I'm no psychiatrist but I'd say a number of factors over the years had built up and pushed him over the edge." He took a sip of whisky. "I found this out afterwards. He started locking Ella in the house if he had to go out, to stop her modelling and because he thought she was seeing other men. Apparently she escaped a couple of times and after that he started tying her to the bed with a pair of handcuffs he'd nicked off me."

"Oh my God!" Indigo remembered the suspicion and paranoia Finn had displayed earlier that evening regarding William and Ella.

"I know. It's bad. Ella admitted to me later on that she'd been modelling swimwear and had stupidly wound Finn up to punish him because he'd become so jealous and unreasonable. She hadn't been doing nude or topless modelling at all. She'd stayed overnight at a girlfriend's a couple of times because Finn was driving her nuts with his endless questions and accusations."

"So she lied!"

"Aye, and fuelled the fires of hell in the process. By the time she realised how bad Finn's state of mind was, it was too late. He didn't believe her when she told him the truth. Many hideous arguments followed. Possessiveness and jealousy are about control, not love. Finn couldn't bear the thought of losing her. He wanted to have her all to himself. He was totally out of control, a loose cannon. Matters came to a head one day shortly after that."

"What happened?" Indigo put the empty mug onto the wooden bedside table.

"Finn had gone down to the Borders to take some photographs for a prospective commission of landscape paintings. He left early around 7 a.m. as it was a sunny day and the light was perfect. Often he would take photographs, blow them up and then paint referring to the photographic image as well as the mental image. He'd planned to be back in three hours. Unfortunately, unforeseen circumstances intervened. Do you mind if I get under the duvet? My feet are like ice."

Indigo nodded.

"Sure, go ahead."

William stripped down to his boxer shorts and climbed into bed. She could smell the musky scent of his skin.

"Oh my God, your feet are freezing!" Indigo squealed in protest as William placed his icy feet on her warm bare legs.

"Don't be selfish, Indigo!" he grinned. "I've had a rough night dealing with a couple of drunks."

"Oh, alright then!"

"That's better." He picked up his whisky glass and topped it up. "Finn was on his way back to North Berwick, on schedule, when he had a car accident. Wasn't his fault, I have to say. Some idiot in a BMW was trying to overtake two cars and a tractor at speed near a bend. Finn was coming the other way and - bang. The country lanes are so narrow and winding. He was lucky he wasn't killed. He was unconscious at the scene and taken to the infirmary. Wallace called me and I tried to get hold of Ella but she wasn't answering her `phone." He gulped his drink and pulled the duvet up over his chest. Indigo covered them both with a red tartan woollen blanket from the bottom of the bed. The curtains were parted at the centre and mist hung outside, poking chilly fingers into the room through a window left ajar.

"Go on."

"In the end I went to the studio. It was mid-afternoon by this time and her green Mini was parked outside. I saw her through the window, chained to the bed asleep, and broke the door down. She'd wet herself. It wasn't nice.

"Finn had a head injury and was suffering from memory loss. He could recall people but not recent events and he kept asking for Ella. He knew who I was but couldn't recall anything recent relating to me. It was the same with Wallace and Ella, though his long term memory seemed unaffected. To begin with I made excuses about why she couldn't visit, but as he got stronger I told him the truth - that she wasn't coming to see him and it was over."

"He didn't believe you?"

"No. I explained why but he refused my explanation. He was confused for ages. He thought that she'd died in the car accident... he was genuinely convinced of it even though he'd been alone. And he thought that I was shielding him from the truth.

With no concrete memories, it was easier for him to believe she was dead. He couldn't handle the truth."

"What a mess."

"Jesus, I know. To make matters worse, he kept forgetting what I'd told him and ended up in such a muddle. Wallace was beside himself and didn't know what to do with him. When he was eventually discharged from hospital, Finn was insufferable, displaying mood swings and bouts of vile temper tantrums completely out of character. I have a friend, a chaplain from my army days. He now lives at a monastery in Italy. He came over and took Finn back with him as a favour to me. The rest you know."

"So Ella did leave him?"

"She was in such a state at the time, I sent her down to an aunt of ours who lives in west Yorkshire. She has a cottage on the edge of Yorkshire Sculpture Park. It's a calm, serene setting by the edge of a lake, away from everything. Ella didn't want to go. She refused, but I forced her. She'd done enough damage!"

Indigo blinked at him. William could be formidable. A feeling of apprehension shot through her, coupled with a surge of excitement. He was so close she could feel their energy connecting as their auras touched. She fought the urge to trail her lips along his biceps and chest.

"Wallace and I had to make a hasty decision," he said defensively. "The pair of them were deranged. Together they would self-destruct. I did what I felt was best."

"I'm not judging, William."

"I feel guilty, yes, for playing God but I knew that they needed time to recover separately. I was different back then. Still sore from the fact my wife had slept with most of East Lothian and I wasn't particularly empathetic or understanding - although Finn is like a brother and I'd do anything for him. Strangely, the experience with Finn and Ella helped me put my past to bed too."

"So are you going to tell Finn what you told me?"

William sighed.

"Yes. I'll drum the truth into him. Do you think that's wise?"

Indigo nodded.

"Yeah, definitely. He needs to know and take responsibility. Then he can move forward. It'll help. It's the not knowing and confusion that's driving him nuts."

"Hmm... No doubt he'll want to see her - God knows what'll happen from here. All she ever talks about is him. Obsessed. And all he ever talks about is her and painting. What a pair! Hopefully they've both learned to grow up and not be so controlling and stupid."

"Leave it up to them then, William. You can only be supportive now."

"Aye."

Leaning over, William stroked her dark hair back from her face and kissed her on the forehead. "I'll not take advantage of you in your drunken state, Ms Summers, but do you mind if we cuddle up tonight? It may be the whisky or mild concussion, but I'm feeling exhausted."

"Of course."

Indigo snuggled into his warm arms. Every sense in her body tingled with awareness at the touch of his soft skin and hard muscles. However, sleep aided by vast quantities of Jack Daniels, exercise and sea air, engulfed her.

During the early hours of the morning, a sea breeze surged into the room casting the white curtain repeatedly upwards where it billowed like a sail before floating downwards. The waves crashed onto the rocks in the distance as the tide pulsed back and forth, and the connection between William and Indigo became physical as well as mental, spiritual and emotional. As skin met skin, Indigo experienced heady sensations she hadn't known existed. Their bodies were perfectly matched.

◆ ◆ ◆

Indigo awoke late. There was a note on the pillow next to her. 'Gone to the pub with Finn. See you later. Wxxx.'

She glanced at her ˋphone. It was twelve noon. Despite drinking nearly a quarter of a bottle of Jack Daniels, she felt refreshed and happy. For a moment she lay remembering the perfect love making with William before reluctantly sitting up in bed. There was still an imprint on the white feather pillow where his head had rested. The indent smelled of his aftershave. Desperate for a large cup of tea, she wandered downstairs. The marble stairs felt like slabs of ice under her feet.

Discarded envelopes from the previous day gaped at her. Taking the post into the kitchen she viewed them morosely over a cup of steaming Yorkshire Tea as they were all bills. The final envelope was white and hand written in dark blue ink. Ripping it open she pulled out a folded letter.

'TART!'

The dark red bold print screamed at her venomously. Fear like black smoke spun in a spiral through her. With pounding heart, her insides heaved. The letter box banged and she visibly jumped. The postman's footsteps crunched back down the drive and the sound of the diesel post office van driving away echoed through her skull. Sifting through the scattered brown envelopes on the prickly brown mat she was relieved to see there were no further white ones. Sitting back down in the kitchen she grimaced at the children's mobile `phone bills. Opening a typed brown envelope, she pulled out the letter.

'I know what you've been up to, TART!'

Indigo dropped the letter in fright. The words were printed in the same bold, dark red ink. It had to be Mike. He was the only person she knew capable of acting in this way. How the hell had he found her? Her mind raced through numerous possibilities. Had he followed her? He was recovering from a car accident with a broken leg and hand so it seemed unlikely. Had he asked a friend of hers from Kent, who didn't know the situation between them? That wasn't possible. The only people who knew where she was living were sworn to secrecy - Charlotte, her best friend from Canterbury, and her children Lily and Charlie. Maybe he'd hired someone? However, that seemed unlikely. If Mike was going to the trouble of intimidating her he would want to benefit directly. He was a complete control freak and wouldn't trust anyone else.

In split seconds her brain analysed numerous possibilities. Her whirling thoughts suddenly ground to a halt. Mike had hacked her email. He must have. She had given her address to a couple of people by email. An internet florist when she first moved to North Berwick and also to the Spiritual Retreat on the Isle of Mull. Her address had been on the confirmation emails received from both. Mike must have guessed the alternative password to the one she'd used when they were together. She'd blocked him and Jeremy Clifford Amos, her ex-employer, when she moved but she hadn't changed her email account.

Mike knew her. Although he was a monster, he certainly wasn't stupid. She should have changed her account or at least picked a random password out of the dictionary when she left him, instead of using a password that was fathomable. Immediately, she tore up the marble stairs two at a time. Pulling out her laptop, she grabbed a novel and chose two words and the page number and wrote the password in the front of the book. Changing the password on her email account and all other Internet accounts, her stomach began to churn with a dark, swirling hatred towards him.

He knew where she lived.

Ok. Well, she wasn't scared of him anymore. He was down south recovering from his accident with time on his hands. He was trying to bully and terrorise her, revelling in the image of her supposed discomfort and terror. While she had hoped that during his recovery he would reflect upon his past behaviour with remorse, it seemed that his foul and violent behaviour was justified in his mind and instead he was plotting his revenge. A true narcissist, she had never known Mike to acknowledge responsibility for his actions, believing that he was always right and everything bad that happened was always someone else's fault. The whole world owed him.

Her first instinct was to tell William and ask his advice. It was the obvious and sensible thing to do. However, she was reluctant to do so. He had so much to deal with at the moment. The night before when he marched them down North Berwick Law he'd looked tired and worn. She didn't want him to view her as another problem to deal with or to appear weak or needy in his eyes.

Mike was her past and therefore her problem to deal with. Picturing his face in her mind, she began to shake with fear as dreadful emotions associated with the memory of their last meeting surfaced. She could still feel each blow of his fists on her body as he pounded her repeatedly until she thought her bones would disintegrate into powder and the stench of stale alcohol on his excited breath as he moved to undo his trousers. If it hadn't been for the ginger cat setting off the car alarm, he would have raped her and thought it his given right. She shook her head at the thought.

Opening the door of the huge oak wardrobe, she reached for the top shelf where she kept red wine. Feeling the glass on her finger tips she hesitated for a moment before pushing it away. Instead, she dressed in clothes suitable for running, applied make-up and tied her hair back into a ponytail. She looked young and fresh but her dark indigo eyes were frightened. If she gave in and became a fearful drunken wreck, then Mike would win. Instead, she would do herself a favour and become fit and healthy. It wouldn't be easy but she had to try.

When Mike came to finish his punishment she had to be ready for him. He would come. Indigo knew that he was merely biding his time, breaking her down gradually, starting with psychological intimidation. When he imagined her weak and petrified he would visit her when she least expected. Only when he'd destroyed her mind, body and soul, would he be happy to move on. She had defied him, wrecked his house and left him. In Mike's mind that was unforgivable.

Indigo slipped on her trainers and glanced out of the window before cautiously opening the front door. The sky was a clear baby blue with a smattering of clouds. The day was mild with a light breeze. Trees lined the drive, waving their bony branches at her in greeting. There was not a soul in sight. Crunching across to the campervan, she drove to the garage at the back of the house out of view then extracted a small telescope from the bedside in the van, locking the vehicle and the garage doors behind it.

Reiki was needed. Negativity from the vile mail, fear, anger and hatred had left her feeling depressed, low in energy and stressed out. She decided to venture to the cave hidden away in the cliff face. Packing cheese and tomato sandwiches, a flask of tea, a rug and some candles, she set off through the cream garden gate onto the compact mud of the coastal path.

The dark blue sea gleamed like a mirror in the weak sunlight, boasting large frothy breakers. Seagulls and small bobbing black and white birds whizzed along the coastline lined with yellow sandy beaches, tired long grasses and cold, dramatic black cliffs. Indigo immediately experienced a lightening as her body relaxed. She had made the right decision. Venturing away from the path, she climbed carefully down the black slate before moving to her right. A large, hooded black crow sat on a rock watching her progress.

"You're not working for Mike, are you?" she asked the sinister bird, scrambling past it up the graduated cliff face.

Reaching the spot, she shone the torch into her haven, a small cave carved into the rock. It was empty, bird and bug free. There were candle stubs from her last visit and half a bottle of red wine she'd left there for a return visit.

"Litter bug," she murmured, climbing into the cave. "Such a drunk."

Placing her lunch and supplies onto a natural shelf at the back of the cave, she lit a candle. Immediately the warm yellow glow of the flickering flame brought comfort into her rocky retreat. She sat on the folded rug and closed her eyes, concentrating on the natural sounds surrounding her. The tide roared as it tore up the beach, a vast energy dragging treasures back into its depths. Gulls squawked, screaming their anguish to the heavens as they fought to fill their great white bellies. Indigo called Reiki and a familiar sensation of inner peace and love flowed through her accompanied by waves of colour. Red liquid velvet pulsed through her skull, soaking into her brain and every strand of her DNA. The image of an almond-shaped piercing eye drifted in and out of the changing shadows as she tended to each chakra. Violets, yellow, blues and greens, rich and empowering, flowed through her. Upon finishing the chakra clearing, she opened her eyes. The seascape vibrated with energy and power as sparkling pure light filmed the ocean. The foliage of distant islands and cliff tops metamorphosed from moss green to brilliant emerald. Nature's echoes were magnified. Her mind and body felt strong, energised and grounded. The nausea left her.

FOUR
The Healing Centre

The cave was sheltered but cold. Indigo ate her sandwich and gulped back hot tea, relishing the heat as it seeped down inside her. Her favourite trail along the coastal path wound down to North Berwick beach but today she purposely chose an alternative route along the cliffs in the opposite direction. A harsh wind blew from the north, chilling the air. Pulling on gloves and a woollen hat, she marched for about two miles before resting on one of the intermittent wooden benches. The golden plaque read:

> *'For Teresa Connolly who rested here every Sunday on her way to Our Lady, Star of the Sea, 1921- 2011.'*

Life's short, mused Indigo. Too brief to waste a moment fretting and living a lesser life than deserved. There would always be people who couldn't relate to her desire for a different way of living. Their arguments were fuelled by their own fears and insecurities rather than true concern for her. Mike was typical of someone who was unyielding. Reluctant to move forward from past negative experiences, he had become warped and bitter in his outlook.

Neat fields of brown and gold dressed the sides of the walk. Stone walls protected the night rambler from plunging down dark ravines to the rocks and sandy inlets below. Hardy green and yellow evergreens lay in clumps scattered at intervals. The sea, a greyish blue, shone under a lighter sky streaked with white, pink and coal dust clouds.

Rummaging for her mobile `phone, Indigo called her best friend, Charlotte. Briefly filling her in on the events of the past few days, she told her about the letters.

"It has to be Mike," said Charlotte in her clipped, matter of fact way. "There's not a chance it could be Finn though? I know you're fond of him but he sounds a bit bonkers."

"Well I don't know for definite but I think it's highly unlikely. He and I have a bond, a friendship. He trusts me."

"He's not become fixated on you now, has he? Transferring his affections from Ella to you?"

"I wouldn't think so. He was mad about Ella and once William's got through to him what truly happened I expect he'll be on the next train down to Yorkshire. He's messed up, yes, plus the accident hasn't helped his mental health, but he's a decent person. Very sweet actually."

"Ok. We'll eliminate him for now. What does William say?"

"I haven't told him."

"He's a policeman, Indigo! He could help. He probably knows other cases of mad stalkers and can tell you what to do!"

"Don't say that - the stalker bit."

"Well, harassment then. What qualifies a stalker? A physical presence?"

"Let's hope he doesn't upgrade from harassment to stalking!" Indigo sighed. "If anything else happens, I'll tell William. I want to stand on my own two feet. Mike's my past and my problem. I've never run to anyone in my life for help - apart from you, but that's different. I mean a man. I don't intend to start now."

"William's different, Indigo. He'd want to help. This could be serious. Mike's obviously a complete nut job."

"I want William to see me for the strong, independent person I am, not some screwed up, needy middle-aged woman with a heap of baggage trailing behind her."

"I get that. I'm just concerned. I'd say come and stay here but I think the further you are from Canterbury at the moment the better."

"Running away won't help, but I feel weary again, despite Reiki. Mike, he knows what he's doing. He knows my weakness. I have to strengthen my resilience against him. Hopefully the poisonous letters have got the venom out of his system."

"What about that fella that you met on the retreat? The one who said he would mentor you?"

"Gabriel?"

"Yes. He has a place in the Lake District you mentioned?"

"I was thinking about him this morning funnily enough. I'll text him. Last time we spoke he asked me to experience an archangel attunement."

"As you do!"

Indigo laughed.

"Yeah. It's where you're attuned to the rays from the seven archangels. Then if you need protection, help or guidance, you can call upon them."

"Well, if you won't accept help from William then I advise you to accept it from the heavenly forces! Perhaps they can zap Mike with a fork of lightning. Seriously, Indigo! I don't need to tell you that Mike's to be taken seriously. Apparently he upset quite a few of the nurses when he was in hospital by being vile and quite personal. He's a nasty piece of work!"

"Did your husband tell you that?"

"Yeah, he did. The other doctors where talking about it in the staff room and Thomas overheard."

A chill shot through Indigo. He must have been really foul to get the hospital staff's attention. Icy claws of fear clung to her bowels.

"I'm going to drive past his house and see if there are any signs of life. And I'll let you know. I would say don't worry, he's just trying to intimidate you, but I'm not so sure."

After the call, Indigo started to walk back home. She felt deflated, scared but also annoyed. Despite trying to move forward with her life the past was still crippling her. Why couldn't Mike just let her go? He hadn't seemed that bothered about her when they were together. Cold and distant, he'd repeatedly torn her character to shreds, falsely accusing her of infidelity, intellectual deficiency, selfishness and manipulation. He had purposely undermined her confidence and worth until she felt powerless, full of self-doubt and depressed. Then the beatings had arrived to add force to his destruction.

He was typical of a person with deep-rooted self-esteem issues who crushed others in order to feel good. Indigo shuddered.

Egotistic and controlling, Mike was being driven by an inner rage and bitterness at her rejection of him. Indigo wished she'd never allowed him into her life. He'd seemed so positive, ambitious and full of charm when she first met him. How could she have known that this would happen? Even as she contemplated it, she knew that there had been the odd comment, behaviour or observation that should have alerted her. Instead, she'd chosen to ignore her intuition and had paid the price. Ignorance brings destruction, not bliss.

Half way back home she received a text message from William.

'Taking Finn to Yorkshire! Emotional but took it better than I thought. B back tomorrow or next day. U ok? X'

'Yes. Glad he's ok. x' she texted back.

Discomfort descended. Despite what she'd said to Charlotte on the `phone about dealing with the problem herself, she'd derived comfort from knowing that William was nearby. But hate mail was arriving daily and now he was two hundred miles away. She didn't fancy being alone in the house at night. What if Mike broke in and crept up the stairs to her bedroom?

> 'Hidden in the murky shadows of the night, he slowly turned the brass handle of her door, creeping into her room like the black angel of death.'

Darkness terrified her as a child due to vivid nightmares and, although she had rationalised the fear as an adult, the dark still scared her. Headlines of murders flashed though her mind. The police said that victims often knew their killer. What if Mike tried to kill her? The face of Rebecca loomed up in her mind and she could hear her Reiki Master's voice telling her that she was spinning with fear. To distract her thoughts, she flicked on her iPod. The song was about a cold-hearted man who ruthlessly hurt women, metaphorically collecting their hearts in a jar without a care... The lyrics could have been written about Mike! She hoped he wasn't planning on literally gouging out her heart and pickling it in a jar.

She was stronger than him. She had to be.

Quickening her pace, she glanced up at the rapidly changing

sky. The previous wisps of black vapour had graduated to immense clouds, smothering the brush strokes of blue and pink, darkening the sky and ocean to gun metal grey. The tide furiously battered the rock barriers in its path, throwing billions of white frothing bubbles up into the air. The wind tugged at Indigo's hat as large icy droplets of rain began to fall, gaining momentum until she was soaked in a deluge.

She opened the front door, shivered and scanned the drive and surrounding area as she closed it behind her. Bolting the door, she removed her wet coat, hat and footwear before methodically checking the house. In each room she looked in the wardrobes, under the beds, behind doors, cupboards and sofas, finishing by scrutinising the window locks and drawing the curtains. She even checked the loft although it frightened her to go up there. The attic was vast and dusty, full of old furniture, paintings and treasures acquired on travels abroad. A forensic detective couldn't have been more thorough than Indigo. Fortunately there was no cellar. Finally convinced that she was alone and the house was secure, she removed her wet clothes and ran a hot rose-scented bath. Luxuriating in the comforting heat, she relaxed following a meditation of empowerment. The steam rose, lifting her spirits and eradicating gut-churning fear.

The lounge provided a cheerful setting for the evening, warmed by a crackling blue and orange flamed fire. Indigo lay comfortably on the sofa laughing through a romantic comedy on the TV. She no longer felt intimidated or afraid despite the darkness and gathering storm outside. Shortly afterwards she went to bed and fell into a deep sleep.

◆ ◆ ◆

She was wandering through an ancient railway tunnel. The arched Victorian brickwork was stained with smears of tar and soot. The stench of stale smoke was rife and a fug of grey fog filled the air. Daylight flirted in the distance but the faster she moved towards the light, the further away it seemed to travel. Criss-crossed rails led to wider tracks and try as she could she couldn't find a way to safety. The third rail was electrified and she was petrified that she would step or fall onto it and be fried alive. Lost and confused, she felt trapped by an inability to move freely or find her way. As she stumbled, the vibration of a train approaching, accompanied by the squeal of grinding brakes, echoed behind her.

◆ ◆ ◆

Indigo awoke with a start, her body bathed in sweat. Sitting up, she gasped into the dimness. The wind outside was battering the house, growling as it sped around the grounds, a hoarse and morose sound. Rain pelted the windows and she could hear the waves smashing with ferocity onto the cliffs. The security lamp outside flicked on, casting light momentarily into the room. The curtains were still partially open and she could hear a scratching at the French windows above the din of the chaotic storm, an eerie high-pitched squeaking similar to a knife sliding down a plate. Two almond yellow eyes gleamed at her through the glass and Indigo screamed in terror, clutching her head. An avalanche of ice shot through her and bile erupted from her stomach, hitting the back of her throat. Momentarily paralysed, she stared into the monstrous eyes. A splitting crackling echoed from within the grounds followed by moaning, and an almighty crash resonated from the direction of the rose lawn.

The wind dropped for a second and Indigo heard a pitiful miaowing and two paws appeared on the shiny surface of the door. A gunshot of thunder exploded overhead and the glaring cat disappeared into the dark night. Scrambling out of bed, Indigo raced to the en-suite bathroom, clutched the sides of the white toilet bowl and wretched into the watery depths, her heart hammering against her chest so violently she was terrified her heart would fail under the strain. Breathing out for ten and in for four, she managed to slow her breathing and lower her pulse rate.

She washed her face and stared into the mirror at her refection. Her face was so pale it was almost translucent. Her blue eyes were huge and her long dark hair wild and dishevelled. Returning to her room, she peered into the night before closing the curtains properly. Silently she cursed the cat. One of the trees that lined the drive had uprooted in the gale, hence the almighty crash. Pouring a large glass of wine, she climbed back into bed and glanced at the clock. Four a.m. - the hour of weakness, bleakness and hopelessness. Texting Gabriel, she mentioned the possibility of an immediate stay at his retreat. Her nerves were shot to bits. In her present state, she was no match for Mike.

The telephone awoke her about ten-thirty. It was Charlotte.

"His car wasn't in the drive. There was a neighbour having a bonfire just over the road. An old fellow. So I asked him if Mike was about and he told me that he'd gone away for a bit. He thought maybe to family up north."

"Not sure if that's good or bad," commented Indigo.

"Bad," Charlotte said. "I would have felt more comfortable if we'd known his exact whereabouts."

"I'm waiting to hear from Gabriel about going down to the Lakes for a few days. I need to get my positive energy up. Feel freaked out, to be honest." Indigo told her about her eventful night.

"God! I'm not surprised you're a nervous wreck. If Gabriel's not available, come here."

"Thanks, Charlotte. I'll keep you posted."

Ending the call, Indigo opened her text messages. One was from William saying that they were at his aunt's and things were going well. Was she okay? The other was from Gabriel, expressing his delight at her imminent visit and that they would have a chat about her problem upon arrival. She was to come straight away. Indigo sighed with relief. Leaping out of bed, she looked out upon the calm new day. The dead tree lay still and quiet in its final motion. Once tall and splendid, reaching for God, it had split, uprooted and fallen sideways onto the rose lawn, defeated by the powerful forces of nature.

She packed her case and decided to drive down to the Lakes in the campervan rather than take the train. Gabriel lived in the depths of the Cumbrian countryside, miles from any town. He had converted part of the family estate into a healing centre situated near a vast lake. She decided to leave in the early hours of the morning. Although it was highly unlikely that Mike was physically watching the property, paranoia urged caution. He would assume her to be asleep at five a.m. Therefore that was the best time to travel south undetected.

As planned, Indigo left before the first light of dawn. Locking the house and garage doors, she was pleased that the rain was torrential. No-one would be mad enough to venture out in this weather without good reason.

◆ ◆ ◆

The Lake District appeared to her long before she arrived. The rain ceased and hills ascended like the flanks of enormous camouflaged beasts of grey and green, merging into the landscape. The sky, a soft mid-blue, was littered with puffy white clouds. Vast lakes rippled out to the mud banks polka dotted with beige boulders, stepping stones for the many birds and creatures that lived there. Indigo reached her destination at eight-thirty having driven at a steady sixty miles per hour down from North Berwick.

Trundling along a narrow winding road with tall evergreen hedgerows at either side, she saw a sign in the shape of an angel pointing her in the right direction through an open five-bar gate. The healing centre was a converted sandstone barn situated in immaculate grounds with wooden fences containing shiny, fit horses and perfectly trimmed lawns. The main farmhouse stood separately to the right, made from the same patchy red sandstone. Small arched windows blinked at her in the morning light. In the distance to the rear of the property, a huge lake glinted surrounded by sloping yellow meadows and looming hills of mysterious shadows.

Gabriel, a tall man in his fifties with white hair and bright eyes, came out to greet her. He was dressed in a strange combination of clothing consisting of a Moroccan caftan, a red embroidered poncho and sturdy black leather boots. He embraced her warmly.

"You look tired, Indigo," he commented.

"Yes, all my good work has been undone."

He shook his head.

"Not undone, just battered. Imagine your spirituality as a tennis racket and that life is throwing balls of negativity at you. You have to learn how to deflect them rather than letting them smack you in the face!"

Indigo grinned.

"Breakfast?"

"That'd be great, I'm famished."

"Excellent! Follow me." Gabriel set off in the direction of the farmhouse.

The thick, oak farmhouse door led to a spacious rustic kitchen. The red flag stone floor was covered by colourful, worn rugs. The ceiling was low, supported by authentic dark wooden beams peppered by years of frustrated woodworm. Gabriel could just stand to his full height without knocking his head. The kitchen units were made of a rough oak wood. The edges of the marble work surfaces purposely appeared ragged and unfinished. An earthenware Belfast sink was sunk amidst the oak and the white goods were hidden out of view. Only a large, black iron Aga stood proudly on its own projecting heat into the snug kitchen. A large, scrubbed farmhouse table dominated the floor, while copper pots and pans hung from beams around the edge of the kitchen. Freshly baked bread wafted to Indigo's nostrils as Gabriel served a vegetarian fry-up of mushrooms, deli rashers, quorn sausages, vine tomatoes and fried fresh eggs laid that morning, accompanied by a warm loaf. Pouring steaming tea into clay mugs, Gabriel smiled at her.

"Dig in. Lana is over at the healing centre. We had a large party of guests who stayed for a fortnight. They only left last night so she's sorting things out."

After breakfast, Gabriel picked up Indigo's bag and carried it over to the healing centre. Indigo wondered if Lana would allow her to ride on one of the horses. They looked in peak condition.

"Tell me what's been happening since we last spoke."

Indigo explained the events of the last week. When she mentioned the hate mail, Gabriel frowned.

"Hmm... a matter for the police, Indigo. It's not just a case of dealing with a problem independently. It's a criminal offence to send hate mail to someone. You must report it as soon as possible."

"I wasn't being stupid. I just didn't want to exacerbate the situation. I thought maybe the letters would've got the anger out of Mike's system."

"Presuming it's him."

"He's the only person I know nasty and mental enough - or with any reason to. If what occurred between us is classed as a valid reason."

"It's unstable behaviour without true reason. Well, it won't hurt to log a note of it at your local police station, Indigo. If more mail or incidences occur then they can investigate - if not, then it'll be filed away."

Indigo nodded glumly, staring into the distance. A bay horse of sixteen hands galloped back and forth, nostrils flaring with his tail streaming out.

"He's beautiful."

"His name's Zeus. He's a friendly chap... spirited."

Lana, Gabriel's partner, walked out of the healing centre and gave Indigo a hug. Small and dark, she looked healthy and pretty.

"Welcome! Good to see you again." Putting her finger under Indigo's chin, she tilted Indigo's head back. "A picture of misery and despair. We'll soon put an end to that. We only have two other guests staying this week and they're a couple so you've pretty much got the place to yourself. You can stay as long as you like. We have a lovely room for you with views over the lake, the hills and a meadow full of horses."

Indigo hugged her back.

"Thank you so much." For a moment she felt choked with emotion at their kindness. She hadn't realised how vulnerable she felt until her arrival.

"We thought that today you could do what you like." Lana gestured for her to follow them into the centre. "You can use the pool or have a walk in the grounds, and Mary our beautician is coming in at five. I hope you don't mind but I booked you a facial and body massage. All natural products."

"That's wonderful! So what I need."

"Pampering is good for the soul. That's what I say. Do unto others as you would have done to you," she chuckled. "Then we'll have dinner together and a shared Reiki session. Let me show you around."

"I'll see you at dinner at 7 o'clock," said Gabriel. "I've got some paperwork to tend to." He walked back in the direction of the farmhouse.

The healing centre was set in a converted sandstone barn. The interior walls were white-washed and wooden, waxed floors gleamed in between the sprawled mats woven with purple, green and orange natural fibres. The ceilings were high with black beams.

"This is the kitchen." Lana showed her a huge open plan kitchen, a duplicate of the rustic farmhouse design. However, attached was a lounge diner with soft scarlet sofas, matching rugs and an original inglenook. Heaps of logs sat to the left along with a big tarnished copper coal bucket. Vast canvases of the seven archangels covered the walls. Red velvet curtains were drawn back from a picture window that travelled the length of the barn. The view overlooked the golden meadows and glittering sapphire lake.

"Wow, beautiful!"

Lana smiled. She led Indigo through another door into the dojo.

The room was large with a domed white ceiling trimmed with gold where it touched the burnt amber walls. Cream crystalised marble flooring gleamed like water. Indigo copied Lana and removed her shoes, expecting ice; however warmth crept up between her toes.

"Clever," Indigo commented.

"The under floor heating was necessary," laughed Lana. "Not very relaxing, meditating on a freezing floor!"

Orange, gold and purple Moroccan silk meditation rugs lay in a pile on the floor, ready for use. Cushions of matching shades lined the lower walls. Large ornate Venetian mirrors hung from the earthy walls.

"Wow, what an amazing picture!" Indigo stood staring up at painting of two heavenly creatures that dominated the entire right wall.

Their form appeared human apart from gleaming silver angel's wings sprouting from their toned, athletic bodies. They stood on a grey slab of stone in front of a powerful cascading waterfall, facing each other with just their fingers touching. A shimmering aura of cobalt blue surrounded the male figure. Gold glowed from the female. At the point where their auras interwove, an emerald energy emanated from their connection. Dark hair gleamed down the length of both backs. Their eyes shone with pure holy light and an air of peace and contentment surrounded them.

"Gabriel painted that."

Indigo's mouth opened with surprise. She had no idea he was such an accomplished artist. The painting was lifelike and commanding.

Mosaic steps led up through an archway. More steps of purple, orange and gold led down to a sliding glass door. As they approached, the door slid back and they moved into a large pool area. Wooden loungers with soft coverings and thick white towels sat around the stone-paved edge of the water. Dark green foliage was in abundance, thriving in the heat and humidity.

"The swimming pool is usually heated to help those with circulatory and arthritic problems, but all enjoy the warm temperature." Lana waved at the still glassy surface. "This was an extension to the barn. We thought it would be therapeutic to have the walls made from reflective glass. You can see out, but no one can see in. The whole wall slides back during the summer months. But we're not overlooked." Lana was referring to the outside wall. Moving to the doors leading off the pool, she showed Indigo the treatment rooms for Reiki and beauty purposes.

"This place is incredible." Indigo couldn't wait to go for a swim.

"Thanks, we're very proud of it."

"Do you own the retreat in Mull too?"

"No. That belongs to Gabriel's second cousin. We just use the grounds. Gives us a chance to really get back to nature - hence the camping. You must be tired." Lana patted her arm. "I'll show you your room."

Indigo's room was next to the kitchen, overlooking the meadows and lake. It was a simple room with wooden floors and furniture, with a king size iron bed placed in the middle. Sitting on it, Indigo was relieved to find that the mattress was soft and comfortable. Cream curtains hung from the picture window and there was a white marble en-suite bathroom with modern fixtures.

"We have four rooms upstairs but I thought this one would be nice and private for you. You can use the patio door to go out if you like. Just remember to lock it after you."

"Thanks, Lana."

"Pleasure. Have fun and help yourself to lunch. Beauty treatments at five and we'll see you at the farmhouse for dinner at seven."

Indigo texted William, telling him where she was and that she'd like to speak to him later if possible. Unpacking her bag, the swimming pool beckoned. She put on her blue bikini, removed her make-up and tied her thick dark hair up into a bun. The pool area was warm and inviting. Purple and cream pillar candles sat in distorted iron holders on the stone-tiled ledges that lined the windows. Indigo wondered if Gabriel was a sculptor as well as an artist and Reiki Master. A docking station was built into one of the ledges and Indigo put on some Reiki healing music. It was wonderful to have the smooth, soothing pool to herself.

For the first time since childhood, Indigo dived into the deep end. The water was heated to a comfortable temperature, although cooler than a hydrotherapy pool. It was like swimming in a giant bathtub. Lana had mentioned that they constantly adjusted the heating setting to suit the client. After twenty lengths, Indigo turned over onto her back and floated. She felt relaxed and free from anxiety. She was drifting along the river of well-being without a thought of resistance or fear.

It was a joyous feeling.

FIVE

Angels

'Now, this is Heaven,' thought Indigo, as Mary applied natural lotions and strange smelling pastes to her face, eye area, neck and chest.

"Is that mud or something herbal?" Indigo lay on the treatment table with her eyes closed trying to work out the different scents wafting around her.

"Shhh... it dries quickly and you'll crack the mask. All ingredients are pure, imported from the Amazon rainforest. They're remarkable products, although some of the smells are a bit dubious. I can't divulge the nature of what exactly my magic potions and lotions contain," she laughed. "But they're all from natural or plant sources."

Covering Indigo's face with a hot, thin muslin cloth, the rich moistures seeped into her tired dry pores rejuvenating and revitalising her skin. In the meantime Mary massaged her head and shoulders. After several applications of different facial exfoliators, face packs, cleansers and moisturisers, Indigo's skin felt twenty years younger. Pinching it, she marvelled how the elasticity had improved. Her skin was glowing. She rolled over onto her front for the massage and groaned with pleasure as Mary's strong fingers worked hard, kneading tight knotted muscles. Tension oozed out of her and she lay there in ecstasy. An odour of lavender and citrus oil wafted into the air.

Her mobile 'phone was ringing as she entered her room. The wooden floor felt warm under her feet as the under-floor heating extended throughout the healing centre. It was William.

"You okay, hen?"

"Yes. You? How's it going?"

"Aye, good. Finn and Ella seem to be getting on okay. We sat down together with my aunt and had a good talk to get things clear. It was a bit intense. Ella gave the scenario her usual theatrics - tears and ranting. Nice to see my aunt though. Finn's gonna stay for a few more days then get the train home. I thought I'd never get him to leave but he's worried about a painting he's working on – the brush strokes are wrong or some such arty nonsense."

"Will Ella come back up with him?"

"Not sure. You can never tell with her. Forgot how moody she is! My aunt's a saint! I was thinking of heading back in the morning but got your message. Didn't know you were planning on attending another witches' coven."

Indigo laughed.

"Well, Gabriel mentioned an archangel attunement a couple of weeks ago and I fancied it."

"You didn't mention it."

"No... well, I wasn't sure."

"So what changed your mind? You weren't nervous on your own in the house were you?" His tone was teasing. "Actually I'd forgotten about Wallace going to Tenerife. Didn't realise it was a definite arrangement or I'd have checked you were okay on your own before leaving. Finn said about it just as we arrived in Yorkshire. You sound a bit edgy - what's up?"

Indigo took a deep breath.

"Oh, nothing really, just got a lot on my mind."

"What? You were okay on you own at the house?"

"Kinda. The wind was mental and we had a bit of a storm. One of the trees on the drive split in half and crashed onto the rose lawn - made me jump. Then there was this scratching coming from the French windows in my room like a nails scraping down a chalk board. It freaked me out a bit. Turned out that some cat had got onto the balcony, trying to get in!"

"Jesus, sorry! I should've been there instead of running around after bloody Finn as usual."

"It doesn't matter..." she began, then remembered Gabriel's warning. There was a fine line between being independent and being foolish. "I was a bit jumpy anyway..." Indigo hesitated for a moment trying to summon the courage and words. "I had a couple of letters that were a bit... I dunno, disturbing..." she began.

"Debt collection?"

"No. Although they're disturbing enough. No, kind of hate mail."

There was a pause. Indigo could imagine William's stern expression as his brain processed the information.

"Mike?" His tone was cold.

Indigo felt her stomach plunge with fear at his tone. Perhaps he was sick of all her problems.

"I think maybe, well, yeah," she said quietly.

"When did you receive them? Where they hand delivered or posted?"

"There was one in a pile of post I hadn't bothered with." She curled her toes, cringing. She sounded irresponsible as if she didn't deal with her financial affairs. "And another arrived through the post on the day you left for Yorkshire."

"What did they say?" he demanded. Indigo felt all knotted up inside and awkward.

"Um... 'Tart'. Obviously a lie," she tried to make light of it. "And the second one said, 'I know what you've been doing, tart'." Her voice sounded unsteady. Heat began to rise up her face.

"Hand written or typed?" asked William.

"Red bold type," Indigo replied in a firmer voice.

"Nice. Christ! Why the hell didn't you tell me straight away?" William sounded furious. "I saw what that - " he swore " - I saw what that piece of shit did to you. I've seen the bruises. What he's capable of. You must know too. What's the matter with you Indigo? You need to bloody wake up!"

"I just felt it was my problem. You've got enough on your plate."

"I'm not a bloody child. I'm ex-forces, Indigo. I think I can handle a few problems, don't you? This is typical of you, not dealing with things."

"What's that supposed to mean? I do!" Indigo was shocked. "That's not fair, William. I'm not one of those needy women. I'm used to dealing with stuff myself, that's all - good and bad!"

"I mean you let people treat you badly. Like Mike. You should have left him long before you did. You let situations snowball out of control."

"Oh really?" she said coldly, her heart thumping with anger. "So this is what you really think of me?"

"Look, I don't wanna argue. Sorry if I came on strong. What's the set up there? Are you in a tent?"

"In this weather? I'm not that mental." Indigo felt like ringing off.

"Of that I'm not convinced! Text me the address."

"Look, William. I know what I'm doing. Gabriel and Lana are looking after me really well. The healing centre's in a converted barn. It's quite secure. I'm staying a few days to sort myself out. Tomorrow I'm doing my archangel attunement and I'll go home the day after." Indigo was infuriated by his patronising manner. "I'm not a child, William. I know how to look after myself."

"Yeah, I saw that," he snapped.

There was an uncomfortable silence.

"I suppose it's all my fault. That's what you think, isn't it?"

"What?"

"The bruises. Mike. I suppose I drove him to it."

"Don't be stupid, of course it's not your fault. I despise men like him! I didn't mean that."

"This is why I didn't tell you. I knew it'd cause a row. Mike pollutes everything he breathes on. This is what he wants, to ruin my life." Indigo sank to the floor in despair. She could feel a hot water pipe beneath her. "Already his plan's working despite everything I'm trying to do. Now we've had a row. I just wanted you to see me for the strong independent woman I am, not some pathetic creature with a heap of baggage."

"I do think you're a strong independent woman. Maybe too independent and no, his plan isn't working. I reacted stupidly, that's all. It was insensitive of me. I shouldn't have had a go at you." He sighed. "Where his type is concerned you can never be too careful. Listen Indigo, I know you can look after yourself but please be careful. I'm gonna email the station and log the facts. Do you have the letters with you? I need details."

"Yeah, I brought them."

William grilled her for the next five minutes with a long list of questions. After the call ended, Indigo felt drained. He cared about her and from an outside perspective maybe it did look as though she hadn't dealt with her problems in the past. Gabriel and Charlotte had also been surprised by her reluctance to involve the police.

Indigo was dying for a drink but Gabriel and Lana were teetotal. 'Three steps forward, two back,' she muttered to herself despondently. However, she knew that the time for negative reflection had passed. She had to focus on positive thoughts, concentrating on what she desired in her life. This could be incorporated into her daily meditation in the form of visualisation.

Dinner proved to be a pleasant affair. Gabriel served tagliatelle with spinach, mascarpone and parmesan followed by summer fruit fool with homemade shortbread. They drank non-alcoholic damson wine. The Reiki share that followed in the dojo fed her energy with waves of warmth and colour, relaxing and healing her disturbed state of mind. She slept well.

◆ ◆ ◆

Hooves thundering around the paddock opposite her room awoke her. A loud whinnying echoed through the silent morning. A bay horse was pawing at the ground, snorting. Sitting up, Indigo could see Lana approaching and shaking a black feed bucket. Patting him, she placed it in front of him and he ate with relish. It was seven a.m. The day was sunny and bright, illuminating the landscape.

A white van ambled down the drive. It was William.

"Oh God!" Indigo leapt out of bed.

Her hair was dishevelled, sticking out to one side as though it had been back-combed and she wore no make-up apart from rings of dried mascara beneath her eyes. Grabbing her make-up bag she tore into the bathroom, locking the door behind her. After an invigorating shower she applied her make-up and emerged from the bathroom in a white healing centre robe. William was sitting on the double bed dressed in jeans and a black jumper, smiling at her. His green eyes glinted in the light.

"What are you doing here?" she feigned surprise. Grabbing hold of her around the waist, he pulled her to him.

"You slept well I see, Ms Summers," he murmured, burrowing his lips into the side of her neck. "You're looking beautiful."

"William, what are you doing here?" she asked again softly.

"Oh, that's a fine greeting." He pulled away staring into her eyes. "Thought we could have breakfast together - you're on my way back home." His lips found hers and any anger Indigo felt towards him dispersed.

After a cooked breakfast of fresh eggs, grilled tomatoes and home-baked bread at the farmhouse, Lana suggested that they went riding.

"Do you ride, William?"

"Aye, I do." Another fact Indigo didn't know about him.

"You're not in a hurry to get back are you?" asked Lana.

"God, no. But unfortunately I shall have to leave late afternoon as the sergeant's already no too pleased at me clearing off for a few days without notice."

"Indigo, will you be okay for the angel attunement about five-thirty in the dojo?" asked Gabriel.

"Yes, looking forward to it."

William mounted a large grey that snorted loudly, tossing his head in the air.

"I can give you a martingale to stop him throwing his head if you like," said Lana.

"No worries. I'll manage. He's no match for me." William reined in the grey as it attempted to cart him off into the meadows. Gabriel lent them both riding hats.

"He's called Storm," commented Lana. "He can be a bit headstrong, as you can see."

Storm was chomping at the bit, flinging green foam from some grass he had snatched earlier into the breeze. Indigo was riding Zeus, the bay horse from the paddock. He was well schooled with a good temperament. Lana pointed out several bridal paths along the lake.

"The first one I told you about through the woods has some log jumps which are fun. Watch out for low lying branches, though. One had me off the other week!" Grinning, she waved at them as they trotted across the manicured lawns towards the lake.

Following the compact mud bridle path they cantered around the edge of the sparkling midnight blue water towards the rustic forest. A pathway had been cleared and chopped logs had been made into jumps should the rider fancy a cross-country course. They picked up speed and raced to the log jumps, both horses clearing them easily, and cantered through miles of trees before arriving at a straight flat run of land stretching around the vast lake.

"Race ya!" yelled Indigo.

Kicking the horses into a gallop they raced together, hooves pounding the ground as the whoosh of air pulsed past them. Indigo crouched down low. They were neck and neck for about a mile. Lather gathered on the shiny coats of the thrusting beasts until eventually Storm broke away, an unchallenged winner. They pulled the horses up to a slow canter as they entered another gathering of trees. The sun shot laser beams of light through gaps in the vegetation. The sky was clear and the air crisp. The smell of leaf mould and wet undergrowth travelled on the wind.

"Needed that," commented William, his eyes twinkling. Indigo nodded, patting Zeus.

"Yeah, certainly blows the cobwebs away! You ride very well."

"Thanks. So do you. My parents first put me on a horse at five and I've been riding ever since."

"I was seven when I started."

William smiled.

"Nice to see you've got colour back in your face. A friend of mine in Longniddry has horses. He's always looking for good riders to help exercise them. Would you be interested?"

"That'd be great!"

They rode for another hour before returning to the healing centre. Taking the horses to the stables, they watered and groomed them before releasing them to the meadow.

"Our turn now." William took her hand and led her back to the room.

◆ ◆ ◆

At five-thirty Indigo made her way to the dojo where Gabriel was waiting for her. Black candle-lit lanterns lined the perimeter of the room and the scent of lavender wafted to her nostrils. In the centre was a thick pile of Moroccan mats surrounded by a ring of crystals. Soothing Reiki healing music danced around, beckoning her in.

Indigo removed her shoes and walked towards Gabriel who was dressed in white robes. He smiled at her and indicated the mats. They were surprisingly soft and warm. Indigo lay down and closed her eyes. She dozed for a short time listening to the melodious rhythm and the sweep of Gabriel's robe on the marble floor. A warm weight pressed upon her crown and heat slowly crept through every fibre of her body travelling down to her toes. Shivers coursed through her followed by a light, blissful sensation. Rays of light came to her, first the deep blue of Archangel Michael and a vague fleeting image of silver patterned wings. Then her mind was saturated in green, yellow, pink, gold, violet and white waves of light accompanied by an outline and rustle of wings. An overwhelming sense of peace and powerful strength flooded through her. Indigo felt invincible, as if she would never experience fear or sadness again.

The sensations ebbed away and contentment filled her as she lay enjoying the ambience. She must have fallen asleep for a short time because when she awoke she saw that Gabriel was just finishing a meditation. Sitting up, she stretched and he opened his eyes.

"That was amazing," she murmured.

"It's a wonderful experience," he nodded, smiling. "Now that you have a strong connection to the archangels you may call upon them whenever you require their assistance or guidance." He stood up and handed her a thin book with a cover of silk embroidery. The rays of the seven archangels had been stitched in the shape of a rainbow with a ray of white light emanating from the centre. The pages were gold-edged. "This book tells you about the seven archangels and their rays, with simple instructions on how to call them."

"Thank you," Indigo smiled. "I feel really privileged."

"The archangels are here to assist us all. People just have to ask for help and it is given."

Indigo returned to her room. Darkness had descended and William was out helping Lana with the horses. They were to have dinner and return to Scotland the following morning, as William had managed to delay his return. She sat reading through the book Gabriel had given her. Optimism and empowerment encompassed her; surely she now had the tools she needed to live her life the way she wanted.

However, the unwelcome emotions of resentment and anger accompanied her on the journey home the following morning.

The image of the brass letterbox at Wallace's house haunted her. She hated to admit it but the letters had affected her more that she first thought. She had felt safe within the grounds of the healing centre, enveloped within the strong positive presence of Gabriel and Lana; but now, following William's white van up the A1, she felt paranoid and exposed. Thoughts of Mike's unfaithful bullying behaviour crowded in on her.

How could time heal when she was still prey to his intimidation? Black murderous hatred filled her with such intensity that she caught her breath. This was not what she had expected after the angel attunement. However, Gabriel had warned her that there would be a clearing of negativity. Tomorrow she would write her feelings down, go to her cave and burn the papers, casting the hatred out of her soul into the universe.

"Shit!" The van swerved as a gust of wind caught the side of the vehicle. Then suddenly she had total power failure. She pulled over to the side of the road, flicking on the hazard lights. "Damn you!" Grabbing her `phone she called William.

"Where are you?" he asked.

"Just outside Dunbar," she snapped crossly.

"I'll come back. I stopped when I lost sight of you, so it shouldn't be too far."

"Perhaps it's overheated."

William arrived shortly after and lifted the bonnet. Emerging with a smear of grease on his nose he shook his head.

"God knows." He wiped his hands with a tissue. "There's a garage in Whitekirk. I'll call them then give you a lift back. It'll need to be towed. You'd better get your stuff out of the back."

They arrived home at lunchtime and she kissed William goodbye. He had to go into work. Entering the house, it seemed big and empty, with an eerie silence. There were a few letters for Wallace but nothing for her. Fingers of foreboding clung to her neck and she shuddered. All was not as it should be. She could sense that something awful was about to happen.

SIX

Attack

I'm fine, William!" He had called for the third time since dropping her back at the house. "You finish your shift at four a.m. I'll see you then. I'll be fine." Pouring out a glass of wine, she sat down on the edge of the bed. "No, I'm not drinking. Just going to bed." She glanced at the clock. The numbers glowed nine p.m. "Early night - you've worn me out!"

She wasn't used to anyone making a fuss of her. Contrary to finding it comforting, she found it disempowering. It wasn't fair to be so irritable with him when he was trying to be supportive. However, the situation with Mike was beginning to get on her nerves. After the `phone call Indigo climbed into bed and tried to read but tiredness enveloped her and she kept reading the same paragraph over and over before eventually drifting off to sleep. In the middle of the night a dream came to her.

◆ ◆ ◆

She was back at the healing centre on the Isle of Mull[1]. Lying on a treatment table in the wooden Reiki hut, she could hear the gentle lapping of the loch waters outside. Gabriel should be there but Indigo sensed that he wasn't. She opened her eyes and saw a figure bending over near the table, splashing liquid around the room. The person was dressed in trousers with a brown, hooded

---

[1] See *Indigo Awakes*.

jacket. Indigo wondered illogically why they were using so much lavender oil. The hut was lit with white pillar candles balanced on log shelves.

Suddenly the crouching character reached up and knocked a candle to the floor. Oil ignited immediately and flames shot upwards, moving at a rapid pace. Fire swarmed, clinging to the sides of the hut, hissing and growling as the dry roof caught. The faceless figure stood cackling with a high-pitched screeching amidst an orange blaze of fire, its fiendish eyes gleaming red in a blackening face. Indigo screamed until her throat hurt, coughing from smoke fumes.

◆ ◆ ◆

Wide awake now, Indigo sat bolt upright trying to catch her breath. The smell of burning had travelled from sleep to reality. The window was open a crack and clouds of smoke surged across the night sky, choking the fresh air.

"Shit!"

She grabbed her white dressing gown and mobile `phone and tore down the stairs, bare feet slapping against cold marble. The stench of scorching wood lessened as she reached the ground floor. Belting her robe tightly around her waist she wrenched open the front door and raced to the back of the house. Her first fear was that Finn had accidently set fire to the studio and could be burning in his sleep, but the studio lay a distance away. It was the garage that was ablaze.

Clouds of black smoke billowed from the roof while yellow flames shot out of an orange haze. Intense heat emanated from the burning building, roasting her cheeks. A cracking sound echoed as part of the roof caved into the interior with a dull thud. The garage was detached from the main house and contained only garden tools and a mower. The fire had not yet spread. Indigo punched 999 into her `phone and gave the address of the property. She was about to call William when she spotted a dark figure creeping furtively along the drive keeping in line with the trees and shrubs to avoid detection. Fury and loathing burst from her.

"I know it's you!" Indigo screamed. "I know it's you, Mike! You coward! You piece of shit! The police know too! LEAVE ME ALONE!"

Pain and primitive rage consumed her and she ran screaming towards him, unaware of the sharp gravel tearing at her bare feet. The figure was about five feet ten, Mike's height, hooded and wearing a black cloak and balaclava. It was him, she was certain. As she ran nearer, the eyes looked startled in the firelight. The garage hissed and a loud explosion spewed out severed planks of smoking, sparking wood onto the rose lawn, scorching the grass. The lawn mower, fuelled by petrol, had exploded. Turning, Indigo shielded her face from the heat.

Picking up a decorative rock that adorned the rose lawn she hurled it at the figure, missing his head but catching him on the shoulder. For a moment they stared at each other like animals.

"You haven't even the guts to show yourself, have you?" she gasped.

He was crouched by a shrub while she stood confidently in her white robe, dishevelled long dark hair, with wide eyes and bleeding feet. She expected him to skulk away into the night but he didn't. Infuriated by the attack, the figure roared like a wild beast. He turned and charged at her.

In fright, Indigo changed direction. Cursing her stupidity, she sprinted across the rose lawn towards the coastal path. She should never have provoked him. The grass felt wet and soothing under her tender feet. She could hear Mike's exerted breath not far behind her. If she lost him in the darkness of the cliffs, she could scramble to her cave. The gate was open and she ran towards it. The sound of sirens roaring up the main road gave her hope.

A dull thud hit the centre of her skull and a sickly blackness laced with white sparks filled her vision. Energy left her legs. Crashing to the ground she tried to wake herself to full consciousness but her eyes felt heavy. Clamps slammed around her ankles. Her body was being dragged. Her dressing gown rose up and bare skin was ripped and exfoliated by the rough ground. Indigo could hear the sound of waves pounding the cliffs nearby. A strangled scream hovered in her throat; Mike thought she was unconscious and if she screamed he might beat or strangle her. Through the gate her stinging, burning body scraped. Strength had deserted her limbs.

They came to a halt and Indigo carefully opened her eyes to slits. They were on the cliff top. He let go of her legs. Weak and dizzy, she lashed out, kicking him in the kneecap. Cursing, he booted her off the edge of the cliff. She heard an exclamation of shock and a brief whiff of lime musk mingled with sea salt hit her senses. Time slowed as she fell...

The night was lit intermittently by moonlight and visibility was dim. However, Indigo was familiar with the coastal paths and knew her exact location. But it appeared her assailant didn't; he thought she'd fallen to her death. A few metres along the path and she would have. It was a short drop and she would hit slate in microseconds. Instinctively relaxing her body, she protected her head with her arms, having acquired this skill during years of riding horses. It had saved her from breaking bones on many occasions.

Pain shot through her as she thumped onto flat, sloping rock with the consistency of a slab of ice. An Arctic chill caressed her bruised body and she lay winded, gasping like a fish in a trawler net. Mike had disappeared and she could hear a commotion coming from the direction of the house accompanied by the sound of a diesel engine and generator. Suddenly she heard Finn's voice. He sounded upset and was talking to someone.

"What the hell - when did you get here?" his upper class accent sounded through the darkness.

"I arrived to see Wallace's garage on fire..." A raised female voice spoke with a broader Scottish accent. She sounded almost hysterical. "Thought I'd surprise you, Finn."

"I've been through the house and there's no sign of Indigo." Finn sounded frantic.

"Perhaps she's not back."

"She is, William said." He swore. "I'm supposed to be keeping an eye on her. Can't do anything right! Indigo?" he shouted. "INDIGO?"

"She'll be okay. She's a big girl. Perhaps she's gone out."

"The van's being fixed at a garage and her bike's here."

"Taxi then."

"She doesn't know many people," Finn sounded irritable. "Are you going to help?" he snapped.

"Calm down. You go and look around the grounds, I'll look around here." The girl's voice sounded annoyed again.

Indigo could see the two figures standing on the cliff top just above her. She opened her mouth but no sound came out. It must be Ella with Finn.

"Okay. Quick, take the torch." Finn threw his torch to her. "I'll go get another one."

They disappeared from view. Indigo gasped for breath. She couldn't speak. Walls of freezing sea spray soaked her and her body moved fractionally down the gradient. Slowly air returned to her lungs.

"Here," she croaked, but barely a sound came out. Feeling in her pocket, she found her `phone and texted Finn. 'Winded on the cliffs below where you were.'

Moments later she heard Ella again.

"Indigo? Indigo?" The silhouette of her head appeared on the cliff top.

Gasping, Indigo waved her arm slowly, hoping that the white of her dressing gown would show up in the darkness. Ella appeared not to see her and moved away again. Staring up at the night sky, she watched wisps of cloud covering the moon and stars. The dark ocean heaved around her restlessly. Indigo gingerly sat up as full breath returned but dizziness overcame her and carefully she lay back on her cold stone bed. Delicate slow movements were needed. Her body ached but her limbs were mobile. A vast wave hit the cliffs, throwing up a fountain of white spray and soaking the slippery slate. Indigo began to slither downwards.

Attempts to prevent her decline proved futile as the black rock, coated with dark emerald seaweed, ice and water, created the consistency of a slide. Thrashing her arms around she managed to grab at a passing slab jutting out from the rugged crag. She hung by her fingertips as the heaving tide repeatedly saturated her. Lying on her front now, Indigo struggled to cling on but the weight of the soaked dressing gown, the continuous drenching and weakness made this an agonising task. Excruciating pain shot through her arm sockets. Glancing down at the churning blackness below Indigo, vowed that if she lived she would never waste a second of her life again.

She was about to die. An unnatural calm encompassed her as she tried to work out her dilemma. Her body felt too weak to haul up the slimy surface, but downwards she was sure to perish in the freezing inky depths. Her children's faces flashed before her and the image of a safe home for the three of them. She still had so much to accomplish.

"I am not going to die," she muttered. "Not yet."

For an eternity she hugged the unfriendly cliff face, frozen to the brink of hypothermia. Where the hell was Finn? A boom and surge of wind tugged at her, howling a morose sinister tune as huge midnight blue velvet waves smashed on the rocks, lashing the land with savage white whips. Torrential rain pelted down like a million pins pricking her skull. It seemed that she was destined either to drown or be encased in ice. Cramp shot through her exhausted numb fingers. Devoid of sensation, her grip loosened and Indigo began to slide at speed down the cliff face.

"Oh my God. No! NO! Archangel Michael, help me!" she screamed in panic as flat slate gave way to an uneven surface covered with prickly sea shells. Sharp edges ripped at her flesh, lacerating her thighs and buttocks. Blood mingled with pulsing sea water. She imagined Archangel Michael's blue protective cloak surrounding her, saving her from plunging to a watery grave or being pulverised by the tide against the jagged rocks.

"Help me, Archangel Michael," she begged, sobbing.

Water cascaded over her and she gasped for air, tumbling down the cliff face and bouncing from iron ledges like an abandoned beach ball. Illogically, she no longer felt afraid. A tugging sensation grabbed at her waist. The belt of her robe had caught onto an odd rock formation weathered by years of angry tides, leaving her dangled with frothing water surging around her legs. She was frozen, battered but alive.

Voices penetrated her semi-conscious state. Torchlight flashed onto her white face and Indigo looked up into a pair of green eyes that were as cold as the wintery sea. A tall girl with long dark hair stared into her glazed indigo eyes before reaching out for her. Finn appeared, slipping and sliding down the rocks, and then William in his police uniform. Indigo whispered thanks to Archangel Michael before losing consciousness.

◆ ◆ ◆

She awoke in hospital. William was slumped asleep on a shabby wooden chair next to her, long lashes fanning his cheekbones. Finn sat at the end of the bed looking anxious. Ella was nowhere to be seen. Seeing that she was awake, Finn nudged William and disappeared to get the doctor.

"Thank God." William perched on the edge of the bed and kissed her. "How are you feeling?"

"Okay," she smiled. "Bit of a headache... feel as though I've got a hangover."

"Probably alcohol withdrawal. You've been out for forty-eight hours. They sedated you because you had a bad concussion." The doctor arrived with nurses and Finn in tow and conducted a series of short tests.

"You've made a good recovery, Ms Summers. A miracle, under the circumstances." The doctor looked pleased. "Just concussion and bruises. You'll need to rest up for a week, mild exercise, nothing too strenuous."

William went out into the corridor to chat to the doctor and returned smiling.

"Apparently you can go home tomorrow."

Indigo suddenly remembered the garage and her face fell.

"You don't want to?" William frowned.

"The garage."

"It's just a garage," he said in a matter of fact way. "Probably old wiring."

"That's not how the fire..." Withering under William's glare, Finn's voice trailed off. "You okay, Indigo? Had us worried for a bit." He walked over and kissed her gently on the cheek.

"Tired, that's all." Indigo could feel her eyes closing. She knew the fire had been started deliberately but couldn't be bothered to think about it. The sanctuary of sleep awaited her. She had been dreaming about angels and a small ancient grey church situated in the countryside by a gurgling stream. Bathing in a pool of hot sunshine, angels protected her with their wings and she wanted to return to their warmth and safety. Hands grasped hers, one warm, large and rough, and the other smooth and soft.

SEVEN

Divine Guidance

Returning home the next day, Indigo expected to feel jittery and uncomfortable but instead she felt focused and calm. Work to rebuild the charred garage had already begun.

"So it was arson," she said to William as he parked on the gravel. He looked at her sharply. "Come on, William. I'm not stupid - and what about the campervan? I bet it was tampered with?" She raised an eyebrow. "Be honest. It didn't do much good for Finn, did it, not being straight?"

William sighed deeply.

"Yes, okay. It was arson, and you're right - the van had been tampered with. Could have lost power at any time." He took a deep breath. "And Mike's being investigated but seems to have an alibi for the night in question."

"A girl, I suppose," said Indigo crossly.

"Does that bother you?"

"No! I mean she's been coerced. He's a manipulator, like most abusers." Indigo glared at William. "Oh yeah, I'm bothered after he's just tried to murder me!"

"That's not proven yet, Indigo."

"Oh, stop being a policeman, William!" Indigo snapped. Climbing out of the van, she slammed the door shut and walked towards the house. William opened the window.

"I'll help you - hang on a minute," he called. "Stropping off... Jeez! Let me help you carry your cases."

"What do you mean?"

"You've been released into my care by the doctor. You're to stay with me until you're better. I did say."

"Did you?"

"Yes, when you first woke up."

"I was a bit groggy."

"That head injury made you jaggy, Indigo."

"Sorry, I've got a bit of a headache - making me irritable. Just wanna be free of him, to get on with my life."

"And you will. I'd be irritable too. Don't apologise."

"Thanks, William. To be honest, I didn't fancy being on my own, not after everything... with him... whoever's still out there."

Stepping out of the van, he pulled her gently into his arms and held her close, kissing her hair. He took the key and opened the front door. A sweet, sickly odour greeted them. The hallway was filled with tubs of Longiflorum lilies. Indigo felt dizzy with shock and staggered backwards. Turning, William caught her arm. Her face was ashen and she felt sick.

"Funeral lilies!" she gasped. "I hate these flowers. Mike... he knows that." She was beginning to feel odd. William picked her up into his arms and carried her back to the van.

"You sit there while I take a look around."

"I need to come," she said weakly.

"Let me at least check the place is safe. I'll lock you in for a minute."

Clicking the key fob, he locked the van door and jogged back to the house while Indigo sat for about fifteen minutes swigging mineral water out of a plastic bottle. William still hadn't emerged and she was feeling stronger. It must have been Mike who put the lilies there. He knew she hated them. How thoughtful of him. Ironically, when they were seeing each other he had never bought her flowers, considering them a waste of money.

What if he were still in the house and had attacked William? Reaching into the back of the van, she pulled a hammer out of the black tool box. She winced and regretted twisting her body as a pain shot through her bruised ribs. She released the central locking, crept to the house and into the hallway. The smell of pollen was quite overpowering. Suddenly she noticed a card peeping out of the array of flowers. Opening the small envelope, she read the greeting message.

'Indigo. In remembrance of your life! I will never forget!' Indigo dropped the card in fright and it fluttered innocently to the floor. Sinking onto the stairs she heard a noise coming from the kitchen.

"William?" she called, poised to run for the front door.

"Aye. Don't you ever do as you're told? In here, yes."

Indigo sneezed several times and went to the kitchen. William held up his hand.

"Don't come any further. There's glass everywhere. Break-in through the back window. Crockery smashed to pieces as well."

Indigo leaned against the door.

"Oh God. What will Wallace think? First the garage, now this!"

"He thinks the garage had a wiring fault. I'm looking after the re-build and the glass can easily be replaced. Crockery isn't anything special either." He ran his fingers through his hair. "I've taken some photos and called for back-up and forensics. I've also checked the rest of the house, including the attic, and it's clear. Let's get some clothes together and go back to mine."

Indigo nodded wearily.

Bumping down the track to William's cabin, Indigo winced at each jolt. Her body was tender and sore. She glanced at his handsome profile and smiled. He parked outside the log hut and kissed her sensuously on the mouth.

"You'll be safe here. Give you time to meditate, rest and talk to your angels. It's a good place to recover."

◆ ◆ ◆

Indigo spent most of the week sleeping. William made her a bed on the large, comfortable red sofa in front of the black wood burner so she could doze watching the flames dancing merrily. His home was furnished in a neutral, minimalistic style and was extremely tidy, the overall impression stylish and uncluttered. They watched films together on a large fifty-inch flat screen TV and went for short walks in the woods and along the beach. Indigo found William companionable, intelligent, knowledgeable and open-minded. He was completely different now to the closed man she had first met who had barely uttered a word.

"This is the best yet," Indigo commented, taking a sip of thick vegetable soup. William had produced a variety of home-made soups throughout the week.

"Made the bread too – well, via the bread-making machine, but I guess that still counts."

Wrapped in William's black dressing gown, Indigo sat back stretching bare legs onto William's lap. Warmth and contentment filled her. Furious red cuts, scratches and gouges crisscrossed a track running from her lower back down to her feet. However, her injuries were healing rapidly in response to a healing cream William applied to the wounds four times a day from a round golden pot. Apparently, the herbal potion had been passed to him from his grandmother who used nothing but homeopathic remedies. Her thick leather-bound journals filled a whole shelf of the large bookcase in the lounge. Each brown gold-leafed book contained details of ingredients and the methodology behind her magical potions and pastes.

Indigo was lucky to be alive. The doctor had been amazed that she had no broken bones, only a patchwork of purple and red bruises. She thanked Archangel Michael daily for saving her life.

"I've really enjoyed this week. So nice to be looked after. Got to be a first. Thanks, William."

"Really?" William looked surprised. "What about your husband?"

"Ex-husband. He wasn't very nice to me most of the time. Professed to love me but it was more about control and ownership than love, I think. He made dinner a couple of times but it was always spoiled by a mood or a problem he had."

"Hmm... some people are draining."

"Yeah. My Reiki master, Rebecca, says that certain people have good high energy and they tend to attract suckers who suck the life out of others around them rather than generate their own energy."

"I think my ex-wife was a bit like that. I always used to feel tired after spending time with her. For the wrong reasons."

Indigo nodded.

"I've been doing a lot of thinking this week. I've decided to sell the house in Kent. It's got quite a bit of equity in it. I've got good friends down south but them aside I really want to cut all ties after what's happened with Mike - guilty or not! I can't imagine even visiting down there now. I'd be a nervous wreck."

William agreed.

"Good idea. There's no point hanging on to something that makes you uncomfortable from the past. I'm all for moving forwards."

"Think I'll call Charlotte later and have a chat about it. The tenants are only young and have a family so I don't want to muck things up for them. How are Finn and Ella getting on? Is she still here?"

"She stayed the night of the fire but left the next day - something to do with work she said. Think she's coming back again. Finn's been a bit quiet about the whole thing. Unlike him. I have a feeling things may have changed for him."

"Really? In what way?"

"Not sure whether it's the accident or his time with the monks, but he seems different... calmer. He was manic when he knew her before. Guess he's grown up a bit. Maybe he's grown out of her. She's quite immature - and looks can only get you so far." He cleared the bowls away and sat back down. "Sorry was that your foot? Didn't mean to crush it!"

"What about her?" Indigo grinned and moved her feet from under his firm buttocks.

"Oh, she's still mad about him." He suddenly looked guarded. "Bit of a jealous streak, Ella. She never really had many friends of her own sex."

Indigo had the feeling there was something he wasn't telling her. A mental picture of Ella's cold green eyes came to her and she gave an involuntary shudder. William put another log on the fire and wrapped a blanket around her shoulders. Kissing her, he trailed his finger up the length of her leg.

"Are you feeling up to a little gentle love making Indigo?" he smiled seductively, planting soft kisses over her face and lips.

"I could be persuaded. But you will mind my ribs!"

William returned to work the next day and Indigo decided to go out for a walk, taking the pepper spray and rape alarm that he'd issued her with. Baby blue sky bestowed crisp cold air onto the Earth and Indigo wore a thick coat and gloves accessorised with a purple woollen hat that covered her ears. The wind tugged at her long hair and barren trees waved naked branches as she strolled through the woods on William's estate. Climbing over a five-bar gate, she stepped into a sloping lime grassy meadow that joined the sandy yellow beach below. Paranoia was her new walking companion. She'd brought her iPod but was too nervous to put it on in case someone sneaked up behind her.

The feeling of being watched followed her although there was no-one in sight. Scrutinising her surroundings, she saw no suspicious figure or glint of sunlight catching the glass of a telescope or binoculars. Maybe it was post-traumatic stress that was causing her anxiety. It was understandable to feel nervous under the circumstances. Whoever had assaulted her and set fire to the garage was still out there.

As she splashed through the shallows in her Wellingtons she let her mind drift back to the night of the fire, reliving the experience over and over. As thoughts came to her, she spoke aloud about how she felt at that time, her feelings towards Mike and how she found him to be a sad, pathetic creature to be pitied rather than despised. She must have looked bizarre to an on-looker but it was cathartic.

Her thoughts travelled to William's cousin Ella. What a strange woman she was. Her eyes were so similar to his in colour but held none of the intensity that lived in his. His vivid green eyes were piercing but Ella's were devoid of any expression. Indigo deduced that Ella was of unstable character. She remembered William's remarks about her jealous nature. The look she had given Indigo had not been friendly. What if William was warning her that Ella harboured jealous feelings towards her - but why should she? William was her cousin. Then Finn's twinkly blue eyes came to mind. Perhaps William had mentioned the unusual bond between them and Ella had taken exception to it. William and Ella kept in touch by `phone and he admitted that he'd forgotten about the negative aspects of her personality. Pure speculation... but Indigo's stream of consciousness was creating some interesting possible scenarios.

The letters with the dark red print entered her ponderous thoughts. Recuperation had brought clarity. She couldn't envisage Mike sending hate mail after all, although she'd been sure that it had been him who had bashed her skull and placed the flowers in the house. Maybe she was wrong, but the spiteful letters would suit the mind of a jealous woman more than that of an abusive, manipulative male.

Reaching the end of the beach she walked up the steep mud path that led to the cliff tops. Clambering over a stile into a muddy field boasting golden stubble, she ventured along a side track. The view of the bay was striking. The East Lothian islands of Bass Rock and Craigleith stood proudly amidst a glittering sheen of liquid mercury and the hills of Fife lay sprawled in the distance, watching the slow progress of a rusty cargo ship loaded with containers ambling up the Firth of Forth. It was then that she spotted a 'For Sale' sign in the distance, strapped to the side of a metal six-bar gate. Hurrying forward, she saw about two acres of land and a ramshackle long farm house sitting back a safe distance from the cliff edge. Her heart began to thump with excitement.

Nearing the farm house, she saw that it was in need of renovation but in a better state of repair than it had appeared from a distance. The walls were constructed from sandstone and the roof of natural slate. Scaffolding leaned against part of the building and heavy duty plastic sheeting was secured to the far end of the roof to keep it water-tight. A long row of out-buildings stood huddled nearby. Indigo made a note on her mobile of the estate agent's number. The property was perfect for refurbishment. The land offered space and a location for both a Bed and Breakfast and a healing centre.

She called Charlotte.

"You sound surprisingly chirpy, Indigo. We've been worried sick!"

"Don't be. I'm okay - just a mass of cuts, grazes and bruises. Seriously, don't worry. I was a bit traumatised but I'm not scared of that creep anymore."

"You should be!"

"No, really I'm not, he's pathetic. I know it sounds crazy but after the other night I know I'm being protected. Plus, I don't think he meant to kill me - just too forceful."

"Why do you think that? He assaults you, drags you across a field - but you don't need to be scared of him anymore because he didn't mean to boot you off the cliff? It was an accident, a misjudgement of how strong his kick is?" Charlotte's voice was agitated. "Have you gone completely mental?"

"Mad as it sounds. I guess I'd been worrying since the letters that Mike was going to kill me. But when I fell I heard him exclaim. He was shocked that I'd fallen. I'm certain he misjudged where the cliff edge was." Indigo looked across the bay. The sun was shining on the distant golden hills. "Could have died that night... but I called out to the angels and they protected me. Whether you believe in angelic intervention or not, it happened. Mike wants to terrorise me but I can deal with that. If he beats me up again before I can put an end to his vendetta, I can handle it. I no longer feel in mortal danger, which is a relief."

"Hmm... he left you for dead... Strange logic! William's ex-forces. Can't he throw him off a cliff or drown him in the sea or something? He's a policeman. No-one would doubt his story."

"Tempting, I admit, but it would be a stain on William's soul and Mike isn't worth that. Hopefully he'll just drop dead." Indigo grinned. "Not very spiritual, though to be honest I think it's sinful to allow others to bully and intimidate. Anyway Charlotte, there's something else I want to discuss with you. It's about the house in Kent."

Charlotte listened in her usual attentive fashion. Her godson and his partner were currently renting Indigo's house.

"I thought we could offer Tommy and Caitlin the house before placing it on the open market. But not sure they'll be able to afford it..."

"I think they'll jump at the chance. I can help with the deposit and Tom's working now so they shouldn't have a problem being accepted for a mortgage. All good, Indigo. Let me talk to them."

After the call ended, Indigo sat on a broken piece of wall gazing at the old farmhouse. Like her it was battered and worn. It just needed some nurturing and love in order to restore it to its former splendour. Returning to William's, she sank into a hot bath leaving the bathroom door ajar. William was at work on an early shift and was due back shortly. Suddenly she heard the front door slam and raised voices. William sounded cross.

"The police have no reason to interview Indigo. I'd taken care of everything and taken a statement from her. Now all this!" he said. "They should be concentrating on Mike. God, I'd like to get my hands on him."

"They want to interview her?" It was Finn's voice. He sounded concerned.

"Apparently there's been an allegation that Indigo set fire to the garage and made the attack up. Basically that she was wandering around the grounds pissed and fell from the cliff edge." Indigo could hear him banging items out of the shopping bag onto the kitchen work surface. The log cabin was all on one level and sound travelled.

"Who though? Mike?" questioned Finn.

"Aye, most likely. You tell me."

"I hope you're not accusing me, William. Why would I want to hurt Indigo? More likely your dear cousin." His tone was disparaging.

"Keep your voice down. Indigo'll be back soon," William snapped. Indigo could hear the clink of glass as he poured whisky into glasses. "My dear cousin? You've changed your tune. The woman you love, or so I thought."

"Things are different now..." Finn's voice was quiet. "I... I didn't know how to broach the subject." His well-spoken voice sounded clipped and precise under pressure.

"You've gone off her, Finn?" William's voice was softer now.

"Complicated, William. We're different people now. She's not as I remember." He paused. "I don't know how to say... I found something in her room back at your aunt's."

"What do you mean?" William demanded. "Finn, what are you talking about?" His tone was angry and aggressive.

"She was in the shower. Her laptop and printer were on the desk in her bedroom. I'd dropped a gold cufflink down the back by accident. It pinged off my sleeve when I was fastening -"

"Get to the point." William's tone was irritable.

"I was fumbling down the back when my fingers closed on some paper that had slid down there."

"And?"

Indigo lay completely still. The intermittent plink of isolated water droplets dripping from the tap were the only sounds coming from the bathroom. The atmosphere in the log cabin was full of suspense and tension. She dared not move for if they became aware of her presence she would never hear the remainder of the conversation.

"I thought it was blank sheets spewed from the printer at first," Finn sounded flustered. "But... shit, I don't want to say this to you... It... it had dark red lettering printed on it. It read

'Whore'... like a practice copy of the hate mail Indigo received."
He sniffed. "I know, it's shocking. She obviously revised the
'whore' for 'tart'... it was premeditated." There was a long silence
as Finn squirmed with obviously discomfort, uncertain of William's reaction. William was trying to absorb the information.

"What?" William sounded dumbfounded. "You're telling me
that Ella sent the hate mail? Jeez, why the hell would she? And
why have you only just told me?"

"I hoped it was a one-off, that it would stop... that maybe the
letters had got the feelings out of her system. She's jealous of
Indigo, I knew that - of her friendship with me and with you too.
When we were kids it was always just the three of us. But then
there was the fire and the flowers and now this. I'm sorry."

"Oh God! Surely not the garage and the assault?" William
sounded horrified.

"I can't see Ella doing that - although it was weird the way
she suddenly turned up that same night," said Finn. "And the
flowers aren't her style. Besides, Ella's not that well off."

"Hmm, I agree actually. I think it's a mixture of both. Ella the
letters and Mike the rest. Mike has an alibi for that night but I
don't believe it for a minute. He's a slippery little shit."

"Do you think it was Ella who told the police Indigo was
drunk?"

"No, Mike definitely. He's trying to discredit Indigo. Trying to
make her look unstable so no-one'll believe anything she says."
William sighed. "This is all she needs. For God's sake, don't tell
her. Look, I've got to go to the garage to pick up the campervan.
It was tampered with. That must have been Mike too. Ella's not
capable and too fond of her perfect nails. Where is she?"

"Aunt's. Coming back up tonight."

"I'll be having a word. Perhaps you could come over and sit
with Indigo this evening?"

"Yeah, sure. I'm gonna have to speak to Ella too. Not looking
forward to it. Can't believe this day has come. Time with the
monks changed my whole perspective on life."

"You're stronger than you think, Finn. Come with me to the
garage. You can drive the van back. Listen, I love Ella but I don't
blame you. I understand, believe me."

The front door banged as the two men left the house. Indigo
lay in the freezing bath water shaking with shock and cold. As

she'd suspected, Ella had been the culprit who sent the letters. Mike, yes, the fire, the assault, the flowers and now the attempt to discredit her.

Her mind drifted to the campervan. There was a campsite overlooking May Island and Bass Rock; she could go there. As much as she valued her friendship with Finn and her relationship with William, she needed to be alone to heal and move forward. She would still spend time with them but she needed to be distant from Ella.

Although it was tempting so cling on to the security and comfort provided by the two men, Indigo needed to find her own way. Their protection weakened her resilience. Besides, she had the angels should she require help. The campsite was populated even in the winter months so she would not be alone. The campervan was adequate to live in until the sale of the house went through. It had a wood burner, cooker and shower.

She would go and view the house on the cliffs. Should it be suitable, she would obtain builders' quotes, make some calculations and take it from there. Easing herself gingerly out of the cold water, she dressed and built a fire in the lounge. She poured herself a glass of red wine and lay on the sofa staring into the flames. Divine guidance was directing her thoughts and actions, of that she was certain.

Indigo was acutely aware that she wasn't the only person with a plan. Mike was in the process of executing his. His vendetta was in its infancy and would increase in venom the more his attempts to intimidate and discredit her failed. He was a determined and lethal character. Charlotte was right; protected or not, she was foolish not to be scared of him.

EIGHT

Dark Shadows

But why would you want to go off on your own at a time like this? Indigo, this is insane! How the hell can I protect you, living on some remote campsite away from me?"

William stood with his back to the fire, glowering down at her. Dressed in black jeans and tee-shirt with bare feet, his dark hair was standing on end still damp from the shower. Maybe it was madness to leave him and the safety of the cabin, but Indigo felt that his strength was weakening her and she needed to be alone even for a short time. In truth, she felt responsible for the havoc and damage her past had brought to pass. Guilt clung to her guts, sickly and churning. It wasn't pleasant to bring trouble to another's door, especially not a kind old man's. If Wallace had been at home the night of the fire, the fright could have killed him. William was paying for the repairs but she was determined to repay him out of the proceeds from her house sale. God only knew what destruction lay ahead. She had to get away from those she cared about before one of them got hurt.

"William, that's the point. I don't need your protection. It's really nice of you - I don't mean to sound callous, I appreciate it, I do. I just need to stand on my own two feet."

"Nice? Such an inadequate adjective... So this - you and I - it means nothing to you?" He gestured to the two of them. "Perhaps you find me 'nice' but not for you?" he added coldly.

"I didn't mean it like that!" Indigo reached out to take his hand. He turned away and poured himself a whisky without offering her one.

"I don't understand you, Indigo. You're so wrapped up in all your spiritual rubbish that you can't see things as they are!"

"It might be nonsense to you, William, but it isn't to me. It's real and it works. Just because you don't understand it or fear it, you dismiss it as a load of crap."

He exhaled in frustration.

"It's not safe for you, that's all I'm saying. We don't yet know all the facts, do we?"

"No, I know. I just think it's for the best, for now anyway. I feel tired. I need to get my energy up."

William chewed the side of his thumb anxiously. He drained the amber liquid in one gulp.

"Is it me?" he asked, placing the crystal glass on the mantelpiece.

The question was ridiculous and Indigo could have laughed. Despite his dark Celtic looks, sweet protective nature and keen intellect, he was full of self-doubt. It reminded Indigo that people rarely see themselves how others do. William wasn't perfect; he could be bossy, arrogant and aloof at times but he was the perfect man for her. In the twenty bleak years of abuse that she had suffered at the hands of Mike and her ex-husband, if someone had told her that she would be having this conversation in the future with a man as decent and gorgeous as William she would have thought it a cruel fabrication.

"No, it's not you. You must be joking. I think the world of you. I just feel weird about what's happened with Mike - just need to sort myself out, deal with the past and concentrate on my spirituality. I've got to get this problem with Mike resolved."

William looked alarmed.

"You leave Mike to the police. You'd better not be planning anything stupid, Indigo... Which reminds me, my sergeant needs to have a brief chat with you about your statement. Just standard procedure."

Indigo nodded.

"Okay."

"You'll stay here?" He ran his fingers through his hair. "No more of this nonsense, do you hear?"

"I can't William. I've told you why. I don't want a row, so just drop it."

"I can't allow it!"

"What're you gonna do, chain me to the bed?" Indigo felt a surge of anger despite understanding William's concern. "You guys are all so controlling. Maybe I'm sick of being told what to do!"

William laughed contemptuously through his nose. Glancing at his watch, he sank to his knees. Cupping her face he kissed her.

"That's supposed to insult me, so I relent. I won't want to be tarred with the same brush as your miserable exes and so I let you have your way, even though I know it's the wrong thing to do. Bit transparent, Indigo - you can do better than that. I have other ways of making you stay..." His lips caressed her cheek. Indigo could smell a hint of lime musk mingled with toothpaste and whisky.

They were interrupted by a sharp rap on the door. Cursing, William rose and opened the door to a blast of freezing air. Finn stepped into the cabin, shivering.

"Bloody weather!" he grumbled, slamming the door shut behind him.

"Bit different to the Italian Riviera, eh?" William ushered him in. "Boots off please, Finn. On the mat! You're trailing mud and leaves all over the floor!"

"Such an old woman!" Finn raised his eyes to Heaven.

"You're early," hissed William to Finn through gritted teeth, as Finn reluctantly placed his brown leather boots neatly by the side of the front door. Finn took off his thick leather jacket and dumped it on the floor on top of the boots, ignoring William's tutting then making a big show of hanging it on the coat stand.

"Hi, Indigo. You're looking as lovely as ever and with a nice bit of colour in your cheeks. Hmm, the way you're sitting there with that expression in your eyes... what is it now? Can't quite interpret it. If I could just capture that... Will you sit for me?"

"Of course." Indigo avoided William's sharp look. Finn seemed a bit wired. Sighting the whisky he rubbed his cold hands together.

"Don't mind if I do. Indigo?"

"No whisky, but a glass of red would be nice please, Finn."

"William?"

"Just a wee nip. Got to pop out up to Wallace's house. Something I forgot to do earlier."

"A wee nip o' whisky on a bitter spring morn; makes you feel happy, relaxed and warm. Nary a drop should ever be wasted of the finest nectar a Scot's ever tasted!" chanted Finn, splashing whisky into glasses. "Although it's a winter's eve, not a spring morn!" he added, gulping back nectar and pouring another.

Indigo chuckled.

"Did you make that up?"

"Nay, lassie. Joseph Wilson, poet. Poetry's not my forte. I'll stick to painting."

"What was it that you meant to do earlier at Wallace's?" Indigo asked William innocently, knowing full well that he was heading up to Finn's to talk to Ella.

"Oh, just police business," he said vaguely, sounding distracted. "Cold out did you say, Finn?"

"Bloody freezing." Finn stood in William's place with his back to the orange and purple flames.

After William left, Finn and Indigo sat on the sofa chatting idly.

"Damn!" exclaimed Indigo.

"What?"

"I meant to go to the shop earlier. Almost out of loo roll."

"Would you like me to go?"

"No, no. You've only got your push bike. I'll take the campervan. Could do with some fresh air."

As Indigo chugged down the track in William's tyre tracks she reflected that lying was becoming a bad habit between the three of them. Parking the campervan on the grass verge outside Wallace's property, she crept to the black iron gates and sneaked into the grounds. The air was freezing and raw as the temperature had plummeted. The grass felt frozen under her feet and the air smelled of snow. The wind was ferocious, slicing at her delicate complexion.

The moon shone a quarter full in the clear midnight blue sky. Stars glittered like sequins pinned upon the dark velvet cloth of the vast universe, marking her progress as she crept sneakily as a thief around the side of the house to the studio. Smoke streamed from the chimney and Indigo saw with delight that the window to the lounge was open a crack despite the icy weather. The littering of cigarette butts on the ground below explained it.

The room was lit by candles and firelight. Ella and William stood facing each other. Ella, tall and beautiful with shiny wavy hair hanging down her back, was dressed in black jeans and a white tee-shirt. She had a full bust and narrow hips. Her eyes were wide with surprise and her mouth formed a sulky pout as she took in William's words. William, standing at five feet eleven, was fractionally taller than her.

"Who told you all this rubbish about hate mail? Indigo?"

"Has Finn spoken to you?"

"Aye, a lot of nonsense along the same lines. He's madder than when he left for Italy. So much for your monk friend, Will."

"Funny. I thought he seemed much improved."

"Oh, I see. A witch hunt against Ella? Ironically, I'm not the witch around here that needs burning – or, better, drowning! I'm to be the scapegoat for a bunch of letters I never sent, am I? She's the trouble-maker, your precious girlfriend. She probably sent them to herself to make you feel sorry for her, so you'd want to protect her. She's got your number alright," she spat angrily, lighting a cigarette. Blowing smoke into William's face, she glared at him. "You're a puppet and she's pulling your strings!"

"Is that what you told the police?" William spoke calmly. His eyes flickered towards the mirror on the wall opposite the window and back to Ella. She laughed.

"No way, wasn't me. Not guilty, PC MacLeod. Your powers of deduction are way off, Sherlock." Ella swore at William. "But if you care to cuff me, officer, I won't object. You used to enjoy that," she added seductively. "You never used to be so hostile towards me, William." She flicked the cigarette butt into the fire and stepped towards him, staring deeply into his eyes. "Quite the opposite in fact. No-one can make you feel like I can, especially not Mrs Hippy with her tree hugging and spooky imaginary friends."

Indigo felt sick. Her heart was hammering in her chest. The old saying about eavesdroppers seldom hearing good came to mind. She began to shake. Ella put her arms around William's waist, pressing her groin against his. They looked like twins. Indigo put her hand over her mouth as bile rushed to her throat.

"I don't know what you imagined happened between us, Ella," he said gently. "But you're wrong." His eyes were filled with a strange light as he glared at her, pulling her even closer.

"You know what's happened... Ouch, you're hurting me!" William's fingers dug into her lower back and buttocks. Her breathing became heavier. Their faces were mere inches apart.

"I know that you're full of fantasies. You were when we were kids. You told your friend Janey that we slept together when we were fourteen, and she told her mother who told my father. When he got home from work, I got the beating of my life compliments of his leather belt, and locked in the cellar overnight with no water or blankets. Do you know how cold it gets in a Scottish stone cellar on a January night? Can you imagine how dark it was? However much you strain to see light, there's none. But do you know what upset me the most? It was your loose gossiping mouth and betrayal of a cousin's friendship. You never did understand the consequences of your actions and stupid fantasies, did you Ella? And it seems you still haven't learned."

"You're crushing me!" Ella gasped. "I can't breathe..."

Steely ice crept down Indigo's spine. Perhaps she should bang on the window. What if William killed her and wrapped her up in a rug with bricks and dumped her in the loch on his parents' estate? Panic began to surge through her.

William shoved Ella away. Gasping, she fell to the floor in front of the fire, hugging herself protectively.

"I forgave you for your delusions in the past because you're my cousin and I love you despite what I suffered due to you," he shouted. "I forgave you for ruining Finn with your lies about modelling and porn. You knew how it would make him feel and how delicate he was - still is. But I won't let you ruin Indigo with your jealousy. Hanging on to childhood crushes and fantasies, Ella, is pathetic! Now, if you sent those letters I'm warning you. Don't mess with me again because what affects her affects me. If you didn't, then I apologise. But don't start up with your lies."

Ella crawled to the sofa and sat down. She was looking up at William under her lashes in confusion.

"Do you understand, Ella?" he demanded.

"Yes."

Indigo had heard enough. Still crouching, she scuttled away into the dark shadows. Obscure black shapes darted to the side of her and she silenced a scream as a large black bat swooped and then circled overhead. Reaching the burnt-out garage, Indigo vomited violently. She felt as though she were being strangled. Climbing into the campervan, she drove back to William's and let herself in the front door.

"They didn't have any?" murmured Finn sleepily from the couch.

"What?" Indigo stared at him blankly.

"Loo roll."

Indigo looked down at her empty hands. The extreme cold and the shock of the overheard conversation had left her feeling disorientated.

"No. They didn't have any." She longed to confide in Finn who seemed so warm, inviting and uncomplicated. "Van stalled a few times by some woods. It was dark, freaked me out."

"I should have come with you. Sorry, Indigo, I didn't think. Was a bit preoccupied. Come sit by the fire." He patted the sofa next to him.

Sipping red wine, Indigo sat soaking up the heat. Finn put a friendly arm around her shoulders and she began to feel better.

"Do you want to talk about it?" she asked tentatively.

"What?"

"You said you were preoccupied."

"Oh... I just had a talk with Ella about our relationship. Dunno, I'm not good at confrontation. Unless I'm pissed on Jack Daniels, that is. I was so in love with her, or so I thought... Then there was all the confusion after the accident, with me thinking she was dead. I had such a picture of who she was in my mind. When I met her again the other week, she seemed different. Maybe my memories are inaccurate. That can happen with amnesia. The patient remembers what they want to rather than what was... Who knows?" He took a deep breath. "Ella just disregarded my doubts. She said it was your fault – sorry, Indigo. Ella's always been the jealous type. She said you're making a play for me as well as William." He took a sip of wine. "I relented, said I was confused and we'd talk more tomorrow and left. Maybe I am. Maybe I just need to get to know her again. In a way she has a point, though."

"What do you mean?"

"Well, you haven't made a play for me. You've been a good friend. But there have been numerous times when I've wished I had a girlfriend like you. You're so genuine and warm, Indigo. I've never met anyone like you."

"That's a lovely thing to say, Finn, thanks. If I wasn't with William and you weren't with Ella..."

"We can be pals. Probably better. Let's toast our friendship."
Finn filled up Indigo's glass and his own. Hugging her close he
kissed her hair.

Indigo went to bed about eleven-thirty. William still hadn't
returned. She'd imagined that he'd be back shortly after her. Her
stomach contracted with a gripping pain as her mind drifted to
unwelcome images of what might be detaining him.

♦ ♦ ♦

She awoke to the sound of a diesel engine pulling up outside and
then pulling away. It sounded like a taxi. It was twelve o'clock.
Her ˈphone was flashing. There were two text messages. One was
from Charlotte saying that she had new information regarding
Mike's accident. Apparently, according to her husband - a doctor
at A & E in Canterbury - there had only been a head injury and
hand trauma, no broken leg. So he was a plausible suspect.
There had been a mix-up with the paperwork. The nature of his
injuries had been bothering her, so she'd investigated further.

The other message was from Finn saying that he'd arrived
home safely. No sign of William but Ella was asleep in front of
the fire, snoring. A key sounded in the lock. Indigo could hear a
shuffling and the clink of glass as William poured himself a drink
and then the sound of him feeding the fire with coal and wood.
Putting on her white fluffy dressing gown, Indigo climbed out of
bed. She checked her appearance and ruffled up her hair before
padding into the lounge. William was sitting on the sofa in his
jeans and tee-shirt nursing a large whisky. He looked tired and
despondent as he stared into the flames.

"You're late." she said.

He didn't look at her. Tension pulsed between them. Judging
by his reaction to her it was obvious that William knew she'd
been listening outside the studio.

"Pub." His voice was thick with alcohol.

"All this time?"

"Er, I saw you in the mirror at Finn's, Indigo, my beloved
partner and trusted soul mate..." He raised a tumbler full of
whisky. "Here's to love, trust and warmth – oh, and spying.
Indigo, I'm ex-forces. How did you think I wouldn't know you

were there?" He took a huge gulp. "I'm trained in... oh, to hell with it. I accept you're traumatised by Ella's accusations that she slept with her cousin. How hideously sick and so Jeremy Kyle." He hiccupped.

Indigo poured herself a glass of water and sat down in front of him on the rug by the fire.

"Wasn't what I expected to hear. So yeah, a bit shocked."

"You'll expect me to deny it, as I did earlier with Ella for your benefit when I tried to convince her she was delusional." He looked at her for the first time. She could see pain in his eyes. He was hurting. "Well, it's true. We did have a sexual relationship for a few years back when we were teenagers. It may sound disgusting to some, but it was a loving and beautiful experience. Ella's two years older than me. I had a crush on her. She seduced me. Half-way through the affair our parents found out due to her gossiping and I suffered for it regularly at the hands of my father. Her parents turned a blind eye. We continued with it for about a year and then reverted to being cousins and friends. Then I joined the armed forces and she went to finishing school. Now we're just pals, but sometimes when she's drunk she tries to sleep with me, like tonight." He stood up unsteadily and poured another drink.

Indigo looked up at him. Despite his admission, it hadn't altered her feelings towards him. It had happened a long time ago and she appreciated his honesty. However, the mental image of Ella and William making love sickened her, igniting red flames of jealousy deep within her.

"I don't reciprocate her desire because I've moved on in every way. I was cruel to her tonight and feel ashamed. I apologised to Ella and swore I would never be so weak again. Then I went to the pub to think. I thought you would've left after what you saw and heard. I didn't know what to do." He put his head in his hands.

"I was in the bath the other day when you and Finn came back early. I heard all about the letters that Finn found down the back of the desk. I knew that you were going to talk to her tonight. That's why I spied on you. I wanted to know what she said in response. She denied sending the letters."

William looked up in surprise.

"She lied."

"How do you know?"

"I've known her my entire life. I can tell. By the way, Finn doesn't know about my past with Ella. Not sure he could deal with it."

"I won't say a word. I'll be leaving in the morning."

"So you do mind..." William looked miserably into the flames. "I can't change the past for us, Indigo. If I could, I would. I can't any more than you can." Sitting forward, he looked into her eyes. "I love you Indigo - I'm so sorry."

Indigo took his hand.

"I love you too, William. But I have to go, especially now."

"Looks like you got your way after all, then." He stood up. "I'm going out for a walk. I won't disturb you again." Dressing in a thick thermal jacket, Wellies, gloves, hat and scarf, he left without looking at her.

Indigo stood in front of the fire, gazing in horror at the wooden cabin door. She felt as though she were slowly sinking downwards through layers of earth into a pit below. A catastrophic landslide caved in the walls to her world and she was being buried alive. Gasping for air, she doubted that even if she crawled to safety she would have the strength to survive a trauma of this magnitude.

What had she done?

NINE
The House

Dark shadows of negativity haunted Indigo's nights. Awaking in a semi-conscious state, she stared blindly into swathes of thick darkness aware of charges of transparent energy surging throughout the room. It had been four days since she'd packed her belongings and moved to the campsite near Tantallon Castle. Imprisoned in a hull of barren, cold loneliness she ached for William's warmth. His vivid green eyes were imprinted on hers and there was an unbearable ache within her solar plexus. Her only remedy was to force her thoughts away from him. 'He's just a thought process', she whispered. If she had amnesia, she wouldn't know him. Her heart disagreed as did her acid stomach. Lighting a candle, she watched the dark sepia shapes dancing around the walls of the campervan. Her `phone read three a.m. Shadow time for troubled souls.

Despite pouring energy and belief into her spiritual development, her life seemed to be slowly disintegrating. Rain fell steadily, banging onto the roof of the campervan like drumsticks beating a rhythm on a drum. Negativity had crept undetected into her positive world, other people's fears and opinions sparking old belief systems loaded with negative thought patterns into action. Her new spiritual life was about positive thinking, self-belief and faith in the higher powers; but she had unconsciously pushed it aside.

Indigo had considered William's love and concern to be disempowering, wrongly assuming that their relationship would cripple her need for independence. It was important to live her own spiritual life; but not to the exclusion of other important aspects, such as her relationship with him. Their worlds could integrate and it was possible for individual growth to occur within their relationship as long as they accepted their differences and oddities.

Today she would begin again. Weeks had passed without meditation or Reiki and as a result she felt wretched and fearful. In times of need, she possessed the tools to ask the archangels for assistance. Despite this she'd embraced negativity, channelling her energy to unpleasant memories of the past, dwelling on her life with Mike and her abhorrence of him. Protestations that she merely pitied Mike were a guise. Indigo hated him and her ex-husband for abusing her and subsequently damaging her self-esteem and confidence, which had in turn affected her life and career choices. Devalued by controlling men, Indigo found it difficult to trust that a man could genuinely love her despite knowing that she was beautiful, lovable and valuable.

Using the techniques learnt on the Mull retreat, she would rid herself of all toxins, cleansing her soul of bitter and resentful feelings. This involved writing down her emotions and then burning the pages, sending the ashes of sentiments out into the universe to disperse. Practising spirituality would empower her self-esteem and confidence. It was time to recognise and embrace her own values, concentrating on positivity and thereby drawing good experiences into her life. No-one would ever be allowed to make her feel worthless again.

Briefly she wrote a text to her Reiki Master Rebecca, telling her how she was feeling and what she proposed to do in order to move forward. A warm calm descended over her. Closing her eyes, she slept deeply.

She awoke about 10 a.m. to find a text from Rebecca.

'You have done so well, Indigo. You are still at the beginning of your journey and need to realise the progress you have made. The old belief systems are engrained and it takes time for the new way of thinking and behaving to take over. It's a reconditioning. You have to remember that others have their own agendas, so beware of that. I have a meditation for you to try, by Solara An-Ra, Goddess of the Light – try her meditations and continue to call Reiki and ask the angels for help. You are on the right path. Let your positive thoughts and dreams guide you. Lots of love, R x'

Indigo took a deep breath. Already she felt stronger. Pulling out her laptop, she typed in Solara An-Ra's web address and downloaded the meditation onto her iPod. Then she lit the wood burner and returned to bed. The morning was cold and crisp and breath streamed from her mouth like a cloud of freezing fog. She snuggled under the plump feather duvet, put on her headphones and closed her eyes.

The meditation began, 'Bring your awareness inside now, into your being.' Indigo relaxed and repeated the invocations throughout the meditation. She was aware of a warm energy pulsing through and around her. The meditation lasted for ten minutes and as it finished she felt refreshed, positive and energised. The meditation would be incorporated into her daily regime upon awaking and going to sleep. In between she would practise Reiki and ask the angels for guidance and assistance.

The campervan soon warmed from the heat of the fire and Indigo drew back the yellow curtains. She had chosen a sheltered hollow overlooking the bay and surrounding islands. The day was sunny, boasting a cobalt blue sky that gave a false impression of warmth. The sea, a lighter shade, twinkled soothingly in the sunlight. Indigo couldn't believe how energised she felt in contrast to the dull pessimism and flatness of the previous day. She had chosen the right path forward.

Her ˋphone gleamed in the light. She texted William.

'Can we talk? I feel responsible... that's why I left. Don't care about Ella. You and I are more important. Indigo xx'

She closed the doors to the wood burner and wandered up to the shower block. Washing the shampoo out of her long dark hair, she reflected on the events of the last month. Again it had been confirmed to her that it was imperative for spirituality to be incorporated into her daily life. Her thoughts drifted to William and guilt hammered on the walls of her conscience. He had taken time off work to look after her, tending to her injuries with consideration and care. He'd talked to her for hours, telling her stories about his travels and he'd cooked an array of delicious meals. In return, she'd left him because she felt guilty and responsible and too insecure to rely on a man for fear of being abandoned or let down. Dressing in jeans and a thick cream jumper, Indigo slipped on leather Wellingtons and trudged back to the campervan. There was a police car parked outside and for a moment Indigo's heart began to race, until she saw an older man with grey hair climbing out upon her approach.

"Indigo Summers?"

"Yes."

"Sergeant Brown. I believe PC MacLeod mentioned I would be calling by to go over your statement? Standard procedure."

"Yes, come in." Indigo unlocked the door of the campervan, removing her Wellingtons. "Take a seat." She gestured to the small seating area by the window overlooking the sea. "Tea?"

"No, thank you."

"You say 'standard procedure'. A source other than PC Mac-Leod has suggested that someone has made an accusation about me." Indigo decided to get straight to the point. She sat down opposite him. Sergeant Brown looked surprised and a little disgruntled. Indigo's frankness had ruined his strategic line of questioning.

"And what source may that be?"

"Oh, I overheard a conversation. No-one was at fault. Anyway, I'm happy to co-operate, Sergeant."

"You say in your statement that you were asleep and the smell of smoke drifted in an open window, awakening you."

"Yes."

"What time was that?"

"Can't be sure but I went to sleep early. I sat in bed with a glass of wine and my book and dropped off after about ten minutes, so it must have been around half-eleven or twelve at night."

"Is it usual to drink wine in bed?" Raising his eyebrows, his mouth pursed with disapproval. He scribbled a note onto his pad.

"Sometimes, yes," replied Indigo calmly.

"How many units of alcohol do you consume on a nightly basis?"

"Two, at a push three - that is units, not bottles," she smiled incongruously.

"So on the night in question you hadn't been out or indoors drinking heavily?"

"No."

"As you know the garage was set on fire deliberately. Do you know why anyone would want to do that?"

"Well, you know from PC MacLeod's report that I filed a concern about some hate mail I'd received from an ex-boyfriend."

"Allegedly... the ex-boyfriend in question being..." he checked his notepad "...a Mr Michael Cecil Barrington."

Indigo's mouth quivered.

"Cecil?"

"This is a serious matter, Ms Summers." The sergeant's tone was stern.

"I'm aware of that, Sergeant. I agree that being bashed over the head, dragged to the cliff top, booted off the edge of a cliff and left for dead *is* very serious."

The policeman cleared his throat loudly.

"So you stand by your original statement and dispute the claim that you set fire to the garage whilst under the influence of alcohol, and that the head injury and fall from the cliffs were due to being in a state of acute inebriation?"

"A malicious fabrication intended to sully my good reputation and character," retorted Indigo indignantly.

"I'll file my report." He stood up. "Any questions, please contact the station. PC MacLeod has taken a leave of absence and so will not be available."

A dull thud hit Indigo's stomach.

"Thank you, Sergeant Brown." Indigo masked her feelings well. After he'd left, Indigo `phoned Finn.

"Hi, Finn. Do you know where William is?"

"No. You two have had a tiff, though, I know that. Are you okay?"

"So so. Has he got his `phone with him and did he say where he was going?"

"No, just that he was taking off for a bit. Sorry, Indigo. I'm sure he'll be in touch."

"We should have talked it out," Indigo sighed. "Lack of communication is such a killer."

"Damn, Ella's just pulled up. Look, she's heading back to Yorkshire in a few days to collect some stuff. I'll explain later. Let's meet for a drink. I'll text you."

"Ok, Finn."

Indigo brewed a pot of green tea. William's ex-wife had been unfaithful numerous times which was a massive rejection for him to bear. Ella had been indiscreet about their teenage affair which had resulted in William being beaten regularly by his father; and now she had turned her back on him too at the first sign of difficulty. No wonder his self-esteem was low when it came to relationships. If only she'd explained how she felt about the fire and break-in and that she was scared of relying on him. Maybe they could have found a solution within their relationship. God, life was complicated at times.

Not that William was blameless. He'd failed to confide in her about his affair with Ella, nor had he mentioned the letters that Finn discovered or the accusation made against her. She remembered the strange look in his eyes as he manhandled Ella. No, William wasn't perfect either.

Pouring tea into a bone china tea cup she breathed in the earthy citrus fragrance. Her mobile `phone rang. It was Charlotte.

"Hi, Charlotte. I was just about to `phone you."

"Did you get my message about Mike?"

"Yes I did. Sorry I haven't replied. I'd completely forgotten about his broken leg, mad as it sounds! Think that bash on the head must have killed a few brain cells." Indigo took a sip of tea, wincing as the boiling liquid nipped her top lip.

"Well, according to Thomas there was no broken leg. Don't ask - he doesn't know what happened either. Must have just been a clerical error at the hospital, he said. You know how vague my dear husband can be."

"You know, I'm no longer convinced that Mike's behind this."

"What d'you mean?"

Indigo gave an account of the last week's occurrences.

"Hmm... Ella sounds a bit mental but I dunno if she'd set fire to Wallace's garage. I mean, he is Finn's father."

"But if she wanted to discredit me or drive me away?"

"Still think Mike's behind this somehow. His house is still empty. According to his neighbour he's now taken 'a long-needed vacation'!"

"The old boy across the road?"

"Yes, he loves a good natter. Anyway, I have some good news!"

"Really?"

"I've spoken to your tenants and Tommy and Caitlin are

thrilled at the prospect of buying the house. As I said, now Tommy's working again they're in a position to buy - with my considerable deposit, of course."

"That's great. But Charlotte, are you sure? You've done so much already."

"Listen Indigo, we've been friends for thirty-five years. You've been the best person you could possibly be - just too bit soft where it comes to these bullies you've been attached to in the past. That's no crime, though, and I want to help."

"I know, but - "

"Indigo, I'm not short of a few bob. In fact, we're loaded if you want to know. Thomas could retire tomorrow and we could live in luxury for the rest of our lives and our kids' lives. I want to see you fulfilling your dreams and potential. And I'd be helping out my godson too. Please let me do this."

"Well, as you put it like that. Thanks, Charlotte."

"Now go and view that house and, if you like it, put in an offer or whatever the procedure is up there. Keep your wits about you where Mike and that nutty Ella are concerned and don't worry about William. He loves you, therefore he'll come back to you."

"Okay."

Indigo felt a further lightening as she ended the call. Her mind drifted to the farmhouse and she dialled the number of the estate agent. They had a slot free that afternoon at three o'clock and would meet her at the property.

◆ ◆ ◆

The house was bigger than Indigo remembered. Although needing repair, the brickwork appeared sound displaying only hairline cracks but nothing to suggest subsidence. Small square windows peered at her with empty eyes of loneliness, aching for love and life to pulse within the cold, abandoned walls once more. Indigo could relate to the house and felt a warm sensation begin in her lower belly. Acres of tatty lime green grass lay between the dwelling and a stone barrier wall that framed the outskirts of the property. Beyond the wall plunged a deadly fifty feet drop to jagged black crags and a swirling angry sea. Another acre lay to the left side connecting with neatly kept fields belonging to the neighbouring farm.

A country road to the back of the house linked the building to civilisation. The estate agent pulled up the mud track driveway in a small black hatchback, grumbling about the freezing wind. She was about twenty and dressed in a thin black suit inappropriate for the climate. Taking out a large brass key she inserted it into the lock.

"It'll need a bit of work - not been lived in for a while," she said, her teeth chattering. An understatement, thought Indigo, as she stepped into the chilly interior.

"The building's not listed?"

The estate agent shook her head.

"No, you won't need to ask permission to do internal renovations or replace windows, which can be a pain..." Her mobile `phone rang. The girl looked flustered and apologised profusely.

"I'm happy to have a look myself," Indigo smiled. "I'll ask you any questions after."

"Ok." The girl smiled gratefully, fleeing back to the warmth of her car.

The building was a strange architectural design. It was rectangular with beamed ceilings. The double front doors were a shabby red peeling affair, snug within a stone archway. Entering a tall wood-panelled hallway paved with grey flagstones, Indigo spied a rustic staircase opposite that boasted a dozen steps before dividing into two staircases leading up onto separate landings. A large, grimy cracked stained glass window gazed down upon the divide, blasting a shaft of light into the house. Indigo imagined that it had once been a colourful focal feature. It could be replaced. The stained glass figure of an angel protecting the house would be splendid. There were three oak doors to the left of her and a door and corridor to the right.

Opening the door to her left she found herself in a spacious lounge with an enormous fireplace displaying an oak mantelpiece and blue marble tiles. The room consisted of floorboards, a huge dirty cream bookshelf covering an entire wall, and cupboards with shelves on either side of the door. There were two windows and old-style metal French windows that opened out to the front of the property. It was cold, shabby and tired but Indigo could feel her energy increasing as she considered its potential.

Icy temperatures hastened her viewing. Closing the door, she opened the next one along. Here she discovered a dining room. It was a bare room with a window and built-in cupboards and shelves. A vast ornate dining table and chairs stood abandoned in the centre, covered by a thick grey cloth of dust. Rubbing the powder aside Indigo discovered antique walnut beneath.

The third room was empty, with French windows opening to the rear of the property. A door under the stairs led to a small bathroom that contained an old Burlington toilet and a cracked sink. A fat, black spider with hairy legs crept out from behind the cistern. Indigo squealed with fright and fled. Crossing the hall, she wandered down a dim corridor with two doors leading off it. The wall opposite must be the kitchen, she mused. Here she found a spare room with one window and a study with a fireplace and French windows. Retreating back down the narrow hall, she entered the door opposite the lounge. The kitchen was gigantic.

A huge inglenook fireplace dominated the room. Old tarnished copper pans hung from the beamed ceiling. An old stone rectangular sink clung to the wall on the left-hand side, neighbouring a black, dusty Aga. A pile of ancient logs sat in a pile, blocking the entrance to the back door that shared the same wall as the fireplace. Three small windows were dotted along the right wall with an old oak farmhouse table situated beneath. Indigo imagined a vast picture window running the length of the kitchen. The views were too spectacular not to be taken advantage of.

The upstairs had three rooms on each landing. On the left was a double bedroom, a bathroom that stank of damp with an iron bath stained with orange, a Burlington toilet and cracked Victorian-style sink. The end room was the master bedroom with sea views. On the right were three double bedrooms, all empty. Out of the grimy, chipped windows she could see an incredible view of the bay. The loft hatch was open and she climbed up the rickety metal ladder, pulling the cord light switch on. Indigo gasped. Despite the roof being in need of repair, the rafters were high and the floor boarded. The loft covered the span of the house. It was a massive space. She could have skylights inserted when the roof was replaced, and divide it into additional bedrooms with en-suite bathrooms.

A stone shed and barn out-buildings stood to the back of the property. The structure of the house was good although the roof would need attention and she suspected there was some dry rot and woodworm treatment necessary. Returning downstairs she found the estate agent shivering in the hall.

"I like it." Indigo grinned at the look of astonishment on the girl's face. "I'll need to get a surveyor round and a couple of builders to quote before I put in an offer, though."

"Aye, of course, that's great."

The girl fished a leaflet out of her folder that contained photos and floor plans of the property, confirming the asking price and how long the property had been empty for. Indigo could afford to buy the house but she would offer a good deal less due to the fact it was a buyer's market and the property needed renovation. It would be an on-going project, possibly taking years to complete; but if she concentrated on finishing the house first, then she could rent rooms out on a Bed and Breakfast basis and possibly run some basic healing retreats offering yoga, Reiki and meditation. That would create extra funds to finance the creation of the actual healing centre, which would be expensive. Adrenalin pumped through her at the prospect of her dream becoming a reality.

TEN
The Ring of Fire

Indigo emailed her solicitor when she returned to the camper-van, instructing him to act on her behalf for both the sale of her English property and purchase of her Scottish home. Her solicitor would provide a surveyor, therefore she needed only to obtain builders' quotes for repair and renovation. He would also liaise with Charlotte to ensure the Kent house sale went smoothly. Checking her ˋphone, anxiety filled her. William had not replied. Panic welled within her. What if she'd lost him? Despite her attempts to focus on the house and spiritual matters, dread lay heavily within her. It was wise to step back and give him the space he needed, but agony when she was desperate for their relationship to return to its previous warm closeness.

Picking up the sales particulars, she smiled. 'Fisherman's Watch'. She poured a glass of red wine and texted Finn, asking if he had heard from William. He replied immediately saying that he hadn't, but did she want to meet for lunch on Thursday? Indigo invited him to the campervan; she would cook them lunch on the stove.

Her ˋphone bleeped. It was a text from Wallace. He was back from Tenerife and wanted to meet her for lunch the next day for a chat. Suddenly Indigo felt mortified. She had been so wrapped up in her own life, it hadn't occurred to her to call Wallace to tell him that she had left the house. It was unlike her to be thoughtless and ill-mannered. They arranged to meet at the Auld Inn at 1 p.m. Indigo decided to cycle there as she still had the bicycle. The wind tugged at the campervan. Hoarse and bitter, it careered around the campsite gaining momentum in an attempt to aspire to typhoon status. There was a crash, bang, BANG! Indigo glanced furtively out into the darkness as a rubbish bin bounced past the campervan, scattering its contents into the night.

Stoking up the wood burner, Indigo lit candles and sat in front of the flames soaking up the warmth. Sounds from her meditation track echoed around her. Peace descended as waves of energy began to pulse through her and she surrendered her anxiety and stress to the higher powers. Serenity filled her as she clambered into bed that night.

In the early hours of the morning, a whirling, hissing sound awoke her. Indigo sat bolt upright in bed; a strange light emanated from outside the van. Throwing on her dressing gown, she took a deep breath and reached out tentatively to the curtain. The noise increased in intensity reaching a manic, hysterical screech. Pulling aside the curtain, Indigo screamed as a glowing eye, piercing and terrifying, hovered in the darkness outside like a helix nebula fallen to Earth. Her heart pounded, leaving her breathless. Logic fought through the fog of terror and adrenalin. It occurred to her that the eye was spinning. Suddenly a shower of white sparks projected from the outer rim as it increased in acceleration. The iris altered from a ring of red with purple and black to red, yellow, black and then finally a fiery glowing red. Then it stopped. Someone had set off a firework. They had purposely chosen the glowing eye of a Catherine Wheel to frighten her. It had worked.

Indigo shook violently, partly from terror but also from cold. Her heart rate slowed but sickness flayed in her stomach. She felt persecuted and intimidated. It was not a pleasant feeling. Her first instinct was to call William. But he hadn't replied to her previous message. Her mind turned to Finn but Ella would still be there. Suddenly she felt alone. Lighting the wood burner for comfort, she sat in bed praying to Archangel Michael to keep her safe and protect her from the evil force that pursued her. Warmth from the fire filled the van and a calm heat crept through her body. Exhaustion closed her eyes and she slept.

Lunch with Wallace proved to be an interesting affair. Arriving at the pub she secured the bike to a down pipe. He was standing by the bar as she entered, nursing a pint.

"Indigo. Good of you to come." He hugged her. His skin was

tanned to a healthy glow. His thick white hair stood on end and his blue twinkly eyes shone with good health. Although in his seventies, he looked ten years younger.

"You're looking well." Indigo felt like a wreck next to his glowing vitality despite being thirty years his junior. She wore make-up and dressed in jeans with her brown leather Wellingtons and an expensive cream cashmere jumper, but she looked and felt rough.

"Warm climate and a bit of sunshine helps. You look tired." He looked concerned. "Ordered you a glass of Shiraz, is that okay?" He handed her a large glass of wine and ushered her over to the sofas situated by the roaring fire. "You may have to pull me up later," he said, sinking into the squashy sofa. "You think I'm joking? I'll never get up from here!"

Indigo grinned.

"I'm sure you can!"

"I was surprised that you'd left," he said, getting straight to the point.

"I know. I'm sorry, it was rude of me. I meant to call you. I had a bit of an accident and I'm not myself at the moment." Indigo felt herself go hot with embarrassment.

Wallace looked at Indigo.

"I always fail to see why young people treat their elders like idiots. I don't mean you, but I got some cock and bull story from William about you leaving and the fire - electrics or something lame. Then my dear son, who is the worse liar imaginable, tells me a slightly different version as he obviously wasn't listening to William properly when he told him what to say."

"They care about you."

"I know and it's mutual. But I was in the military for forty-odd years. I'm by no means faint-hearted. I thought to myself, Indigo will treat me as an equal and give me the truth."

"Crafty," Indigo laughed. "The boys'll kill me."

"I won't tell."

Indigo took a long drink and told him the events of the past few weeks, adding how she felt about the situation with William. Wallace rubbed his eyebrow and took a sip of his pint.

"You have an enemy, for sure. Question is, who and why?"

"You don't think it's Mike?"

"I wish I could say yes, because then it wouldn't be one of the other three."

Indigo was shocked.

"William, Ella or Finn?" She put her glass down onto the oak table. "Surely you wouldn't suspect your own son, Wallace? He's such a sweetie…"

"You've forgotten his behaviour before the car accident. I love Finn and, yes, he's a talented and sweet boy - but he inherited his mother's neurotic nature, sadly. Sometimes he's fine and but then he has a bout of madness. It's the only way to describe it."

"I can't believe he'd harm me."

"Normally he wouldn't, but it depends what's going on in his mind. What's driving him. I'm not convinced by this miraculous recovery. William thinks his time with the monks has changed him. Maybe it has calmed him but William doesn't have any knowledge of these matters or understand them. I would be amazed if William was behind any of this business with you, though. It goes against everything that he believes in."

"Are you suggesting Finn's schizophrenic?"

"No… possibly verging on it, only sometimes. It seems to be triggered by stress."

"Oh," said Indigo gloomily. "He does seem a bit paranoid." She told Wallace about his accusations towards William when they had been drunk at the top of the Law. "Mind you," she added heatedly, "knowing now what I do about William and Ella's affair, maybe there was some truth in the accusation that William wanted Finn out of the way?" She glanced at Wallace warily. Careless words had fallen from her lips. Did he know about the teenage romance?

"William's had plenty of opportunity when Finn was in Italy if he wanted to rekindle that affair. That died a death a long time ago for him. It was a crush. A young lad seduced by an older, very beautiful girl. That's all."

"What about Ella in all this?" Indigo relaxed with relief. She would have to be more discreet in future.

"She was always strange, even as a child." He picked up the menu. "She adored William and Finn. The three of them were inseparable in the school holidays. But she had such a jealous streak - so who knows? Perhaps I shouldn't have sent Finn to boarding school. Ruby was never there for him and he was such a different child, I didn't know how to deal with him. Pity we're not born with the knowledge we have in our winter years. We have to learn the hard way..."

"I know. I think Finn would have struggled with school wherever he went. All he's interested in is his art. Was he like that as a child?"

Wallace nodded.

"He would have these strange abstract moods where no-one could penetrate his armour. He'd go off for hours to the beach or up the Law with his sketch pad and a little watercolour set. He'd come back and give me paintings of seascapes or plants that brought tears to my eyes, they were so beautiful and exact. I've kept them all. They're in a trunk in the attic. He'd say, 'Don't think I'm not happy, Dad. I just like different things to the other boys'." He blew his nose loudly on a large cotton handkerchief. "I couldn't see how he preferred his own company but he seemed to. Not to say he didn't have friends, but just a handful. Are you hungry?"

"Peckish, yes."

They sat eating thick lentil soup with buttered oatcakes. Wallace ordered coffee. Indigo told him about Fisherman's Watch.

"Sounds great. Pleased for you. I'd love to see it. Will you come back for a while or are you happy in the campervan?"

"Think it's best for now. Hopefully the sale will go through quickly. What are you up to?"

"Well, problem-solving for the local council. You know I sit on the Board. We have a putting green, down by the beach, but they want something new and different to go next to it. Big expanse of lawn going to waste."

"I was surprised there's not a crazy golf course in North Berwick."

"Go on." Wallace looked interested.

"Well, I expected there to be a themed crazy golf course for kids and visitors, featuring all North Berwick has to offer. Funnily enough, the other day I was thinking of business ideas and it occurred to me what a hit it would be, especially with the tourists. The first base could be the Bass Rock - a mini model. The golfer has to send his ball along a wave up to the top of the giant's white head where the ball rolls down through the lighthouse and plops down a wave to the other side."

"Second base?"

"The Law. The golfer hits the ball up to the summit and it rolls down like a helter-skelter, weaving in and out of bushes and rocks. Third, the Seabird Centre, you hit the ball through the Centre into the beak of a puffin or gull then the ball emerges like a laid egg! Fourth is Fidra or Treasure Island - the ball is hit onto the island and it would roll down around the lighthouse. There could be a pirate with a wooden leg, lying down on the rocks, and the ball would roll into his open mouth out through his wooden leg into a treasure chest before landing on a large book. Here the ball interweaves through some of Robert Louis Stevenson's actual text embossed in gold from the story. Then there could be a row of boats giving trips to the Bass Rock and Fidra and the golfer would have to shoot the ball through the bows, that sort of thing..."

Wallace looked thrilled.

"I feel quite excited," he said. "Could you sketch these?"

"No, I'm terrible at drawing even though I enjoy it. But I know a man who can and we're meeting for lunch tomorrow. I'll write some text to go with each to explain the concept and instructions - we'd need a few other bases but I'm sure we could think of something. I know - Tantallon Castle, up the slope to the battlements and ping down to the ruins below."

"Excellent." Wallace rubbed his hands together. "Ha ha, this'll wipe the smug look of Jim Macduff's face. He wants it made into a garden to sit in. There are enough places to sit. We could add a few benches, though - memorial benches and flowers around the edges of the course. Hmm, he couldn't argue then, could he?"

Indigo returned to the campervan feeling happy and optimistic. Lighting the wood burner, she sat drawing rough sketches to show Finn and writing clear text beneath each. As the van warmed she felt relaxed and happy. It was then that she noticed a white envelope had been pushed under the door, partly obscured by the door mat. Dread filled her as she picked it up. It was hand written.

'To whom it may concern. We have received complaints from holiday makers/residents that you have been setting off fireworks late at night. Fireworks are strictly forbidden, especially at a late hour. Should this happen again you will be asked to leave. John Broadbent, Site Manager.'

Fury filled Indigo. What a cheek! She was the one being terrorised in the early hours by fiery eyes burning in the darkness and yet here was a written warning addressed to her. This was

Mike's plan – or whoever's - to discredit her wherever she went and to cause as much disruption as possible.

'One step forward, three back', she muttered later, clambering into bed having returned from the campsite office. Her letter was waiting for the attention of Mr Broadbent denying responsibility for the offending firework. She was the victim, not the perpetrator. Indigo felt wound up and twitchy. Lying in bed, she chose one of the meditation tracks to ground her. Relaxation engulfed her by the time she reached the third track.

That night she dreamed of the fire. This time though, Wallace's house was on fire with pointed orange and purple flames shooting up through the roof, burning the attic and all his precious memories. Awaking with a start, Indigo could smell burning. Leaping out of bed, she fought through the watery sleep in her eyes desperately attempting to focus. The wood burner was safe, just glowing red embers twinkling in the iron tray. Glancing outside, she saw the grass was on fire. Indigo swore, put on her dressing gown and grabbed the fire extinguisher from the wall. Anger surged through her as she pulled open the door. The night was bitter cold with a clear black sky full of tiny golden stars. For a second she gazed at the orange ring of fire circling the van before extinguishing the flames.

Her bare legs were icy as she put a pan of hot milk and cocoa onto the stove, relighting the wood burner. Tomorrow, after the lunch with Finn, she would leave this place. Her mind drifted to the parking spot by the cliffs where she had first met William. No-one was bothered about campervans parked there, not this time of year. William was probably just being fastidious when he'd told her to move on that night. Yes, she would go there until her house purchase went through.

Adding sugar, she stirred the brown liquid thoughtfully. Her previous confusion had passed. Indigo was now convinced that it was Mike executing the vendetta against her and not one of the other three. He was her past and part of a negative state of being. Although she was still healing, Wallace, William and Finn were part of her new, positive life. Her association with them had brought good things to her life. The room at Wallace's had enabled her to develop a relationship with William and a friendship with Wallace and Finn. Ella had created complications but those problems had pushed William and her together. Ella had her own journey and issues to deal with. Indigo believed that she had sent the letters out of jealousy, but that was all she was guilty of.

Tomorrow she would secretly drive to her new location and keep moving to different parking places, taking care to ensure that she wasn't followed. No doubt there would be complaints from the other residents of the campsite the next day due to the night's activities. The ring of fire was a brazen act of war. It was the deed of a bully with no respect, symbolic of Mike's assumed victory: "I've won. You're trapped. Give up," it said. Indigo couldn't deny that the nightly events frightened her, but she was seething with rage that he was continuing to abuse her from afar.

"Anger's good," she muttered to herself. Her thoughts kept moving from the fire to William. Where was he? She needed him. But then she had rejected his protection. Mike came to her mind. She remembered going to his house one autumn evening before moving in with him. He was busy throwing huge branches onto a bonfire in the back garden from dead trees and shrubs he'd spent the day clearing. Shaking lighter fluid on the mass of vegetation, he ignited it, delighting in the roar and upsurge of fire that burned synthetically until eventually catching the damp rotten wood.

"Fire brings out the most primitive instincts known to man," he'd yelled, dancing around the orange blaze, whooping. "Can't beat it!"

Peeking through the curtains for reassurance, dark sinister shapes shifted in the dimness. Indigo shuddered and whispered a prayer to Archangel Michael. All the acts against her had included the element of fire - the garage, the firework, now the ring of fire. Indigo did not intend to be the loser in the war Mike had declared on her. He might have the evil fires of hell on his side, but she had an army of angels on hers.

ELEVEN

Cutting Cords

The fresh blue glow of dawn slipped under the yellow curtains, bringing relief to Indigo who'd barely slept. Most of the night had been spent trying to transform fearful thoughts into positive ones whilst peeping out of the curtains into the dimness of the early hours of the morning. It may have been her imagination but she kept seeing dark shadows rustling past the van, swooping in the darkness. The image of a cloaked figure haunted her. The day arrived sunny, cold and bright. The sea glittered like a trillion sapphires spread out upon the Earth. The shrill clacking of seagulls echoed on a breeze laced with sea salt.

Her night of fright and unrest left her tired and tearful. She debated whether to cancel her lunch with Finn but procrastination and avoidance would not help. Besides, Wallace was counting on the drawings being ready for his council meeting the following Monday. She would not let him down again.

Paranoid thoughts infected her as she headed to the shower block, convinced that the eyes of the campsite were upon her. Her fellow campers were sure to be discussing her weird antics and waiting for their chance to inform Mr Broadbent of her latest transgression. Standing in the shower, hot water massaged her tense muscles. Indigo felt anxiety clawing at her stomach; she would have to toughen up if she were going to survive, let alone beat Mike at his cruel game.

Maybe a private investigator was the answer. She could hire someone to follow Mike and maybe Ella, Finn and William too.

But how much would that cost? Perhaps she could do the investigating. But what if they were stalking her at the same time? A cartoon sketch appeared in Indigo's head of the five of them all bent double like Sherlock Holmes with a magnifying glass, secretly following each other around North Berwick in a big circle, and she began to laugh. Suddenly life seemed less depressing.

Dressing in black tights, boots and a short skirt she added the cashmere jumper from the previous day. Applying make-up and drying her long dark hair, she looked almost normal. Her dark indigo eyes were huge in her pale worn face. She cursed the fine lines around her eyes as she marched back to the camper-van, purposely avoiding eye contact with anyone from the other caravans.

Cooking was therapeutic and she had chosen a lunch of monkfish in lemon butter wine sauce. Sitting on the bed reading through the recipe, she jumped at a loud rap on the door. Glancing through a crack in the net curtains she saw a small overweight man with a bald head and bad tempered expression on his red face. It had to be Broadbent, the Site Manager. Indigo ducked down to the floor. He rapped again and then there was the sound of paper being pushed under the door. After he'd left she picked up the letter.

'To Ms Summers. I believe you are the owner of this van. Despite a previous warning, you have continued to disobey the terms and conditions of the campsite and we have no choice other than to ask you to leave by six o'clock this evening. No refund will be given. John Broadbent, Site Manger.'

Indigo ripped the letter to pieces and fed it to the wood burner, ranting about what John Broadbent could do with his terms and conditions. Being asked to leave wasn't a major disruption as she had planned to go anyway, but it was humiliating. Taking a swig of white wine out of the bottle, she grimaced. It was unpleasant being talked about and she didn't like it. Being judged by others as a troublemaker was horrible. They had ganged up on her in order to remove her from the site. Indigo was the victim of a witch hunt. She felt exposed and uncomfortable like an escaped criminal. Wherever she rested, trouble came to her and she had to move on. Mike's meddling was proving fruitful so far. It was time to put an end to it.

As soon as the purchase of Fisherman's Watch was complete she could live without disturbance, no longer obliged to mix with anyone she didn't want to. At least she had the luxury of being able to buy her own home, which was a privilege in the current economic climate.

Heating the pan, she added the monkfish and shook salt and pepper over the top. Music was needed. She chose a rock album from her iPod. She swayed her hips to the rhythm as she placed sticks of butter on top of the fish before adding white wine, lemon juice and diced parsley. Putting the lid on the pan, she fixed the timer for thirty minutes and set the table.

Finn arrived promptly. He looked tall and handsome, dressed in black jeans and a dark charcoal grey shirt. His blond hair stood on end, flopping onto his forehead. His blue eyes sparkled like the ocean behind him.

"Come in," Indigo greeted him enthusiastically with a hug. He thrust a bottle of champagne at her.

They sat at the small table drinking the champagne, deep in conversation regarding the crazy golf course. Finn flicked through her sketches and instructions. He took a slug of champagne.

"I'll have these ready by Monday, no probs. I must say I like your ideas. I think Treasure Island could be more of a feature. The golfer could literally stand on the model island to put the ball through the pirate's mouth. The scale of the models will have to be discussed..."

"Brilliant! I agree. Knew you'd have ideas of your own."

Finn grinned. A delicious aroma of lemon, wine and monkfish wafted from the pan.

"So what's your news? Last time we spoke you said you weren't sure how you felt about Ella, and the next thing she's going down to Yorkshire to get more stuff."

Finn rubbed his forehead with his fingertips. His nails were perfectly manicured but there was a stain of oil paint that he'd missed on the side of his hand.

"I know... I'm a bit confused, to be honest. Ella can be very persuasive when she wants something. I thought... oh, what the hell, just see how it goes."

Indigo nodded.

"She wouldn't have hurt you, Indigo," he added cautiously. "I know she's done wrong with those malicious letters, but the fire and the rest of it - no way. She would know that it'd upset my Dad and she's no psycho, despite her faults. I still haven't forgiven her for the letters - told her I was disappointed in her and she started crying."

Indigo felt no sympathy for Ella. She was a selfish, stupid and cold-hearted woman in her opinion. Not a very spiritual summary but an accurate one. The bleeper went off and she served the fish with rocket and baby leafed spinach, washed down with white wine.

"Nice wine."

"Yes." Indigo picked up the bottle and read from the label on the back. "Tocai is a fruity white wine from the Fruili region of north-eastern Italy. Food pairings: monkfish and seafood."

"Very impressive, Ms Summers." Finn took another sip. "You really are a lady of many talents. This food is delicious."

"I aim to please." She smiled at Finn and their eyes locked for a moment. Indigo suddenly felt awkward. There was no doubt that Finn was attracted to her. She could tell by the way he was looking at her. It was a complication neither of them needed.

"That's one of the differences I like about you, Indigo," he said. "All the women I've ever known have been completely self-absorbed. You're different."

"Oh, I can assure you, Finn, I spend a lot of time being introspective!"

"But you think of others too, constantly." He smiled. "Thanks for a lovely meal. You did well." Leaning forward, he smoothed a strand of dark hair back from her forehead and kissed her gently on the mouth. He stood up and began clearing the dishes into the tiny sink. "You sit there while I wash up." He squirted lemon washing up liquid over the dishes.

Finn's lips had felt soft and warm. Indigo was surprised by the volt of desire that shot through her. William had been absent for under a week and already her disloyal body was responding to the touch of another man. Finn was tactile by nature, therefore it was wise not to read too much into the gentle kiss. The sooner she got away on her own the better. Finn was vulnerable and so was she. Unstable mental and emotional states were breeding grounds for indulging sexual impulses. She needed comfort but having sex with Finn, although no doubt pleasurable, was not the answer. William would never forgive her and it would be the end for them.

After sitting drinking coffee and chatting idly, Finn got up to go. Gathering up the sketches for the golf course, he pulled Indigo off the seat into his arms and hugged her. She could smell the subtle odour of his expensive aftershave and body scent. His chest muscles felt hard against her cheek. His hand caressed her scalp. Gently taking a handful of her hair, he tilted her head back and kissed her properly, ignoring her weak protests. Letting go, he looked down at her.

"Sorry, I've just always wanted to do that. You're so beautiful, Indigo." He stroked her face. "Forgive me. I'll text you and let you know how I'm doing with the sketches. Thanks again for lunch." His breathing was uneven as he attempted to regain control of himself.

Indigo kept her emotions firmly to herself. She was appalled by how much she wanted him. What was wrong with her? She didn't trust herself to speak. Finn looked anxious.

"Am I forgiven? It won't happen again."

Indigo nodded.

"It can't... what about William... and Ella for that matter?" Her voice sounded strained and tight.

"I know. I do. I'll go get on with these. We're okay?"

"Yes. Pals."

After he left, Indigo sank to the floor in front of the wood burner clutching her head in her hands. She was more on the edge than she'd realised. One thing the kiss told her was that she had to be careful. Her emotions were in tatters. She loved William but she was in danger of making stupid mistakes and ruining their future relationship. She was aware of her growing attraction to Finn, who was there when she needed him in the absence of William.

It was time to cut all cords.

At five minutes to six, a defiant Indigo drove from the campsite. The stay had been disastrous and she felt hot with mortification as she saw curtains twitching. She had to keep in mind that she was not guilty and that the other campers didn't know the facts. Ten minutes later she arrived at her new parking place, satisfied that no-one had followed her. Arriving by the cliffs on the outskirts of North Berwick town, she spotted a lower and more secluded parking spot right by the cliff wall. It had an overhang and offered shelter from the wind.

Indigo manoeuvred the van into the spot. There was no-one about, not even a dog walker. The water tank was still exposed enough to collect rain water but with no electricity she would have to use the generator in order to shower. Candles would be cosier for lighting and she had the wood burner for heat. There was no Internet access but she would manage as her emails came through to her ˙phone. It was nice to be near the sea despite the bitter north wind that was already battering the coast. Fiddling with her ˙phone, she wondered whether or not to call William. Pride prevented her. Placing one of the long seat cushions on the floor in front of the wood burner, she lay enjoying the welcome flames of comfort and warmth.

It wasn't worth dwelling upon the kiss with Finn. It had been a one-off and should be placed in a box of memories. Finn was unique. He was almost childlike in the way he gave in to his impulses and desires without a second thought. He'd wanted to kiss Indigo out of desire and curiosity, therefore he had. A charming and enthusiastic character, he'd embraced the crazy golf idea with excitement. He, like his father, loved a project and a challenge.

As she drifted to sleep, a male voice began speaking to her through her dreams. She strained to hear what he was saying. It must be an angel, she thought. Perhaps it was Archangel Michael. How strange that he was Scottish; she had never considered that the angels would have a particular way of speaking. The voice grew louder. Opening her eyes, Indigo screamed in fright. A dark figure loomed in the doorway of the campervan. Mike, tired of games, had come to finish what he'd started on the cliffs. Her screaming grew louder as disorientation swamped her.

"What the hell, Indigo - it's me, William." Slamming the door shut behind him, he grabbed hold of her. Confusion swirled around her. Was she asleep or awake? Her heart hammered at the walls of her chest. "Stop screaming, Indigo, it's me." His tone was stern. "You're hysterical." Indigo felt a slap and sting on her cheek and awoke properly. William was kneeling beside her. Indigo burst into tears. He sat down on the floor next to her and pulled her into his arms, cradled her sobbing form.

"Shhh, shhh... although you're lucky it was me - an open invitation to Mike, leaving the door unlocked. What were you thinking?"

"Oh God, William, I was so scared. I thought it was him, thought he'd come to kill me. I just lay down for a doze." She couldn't stop crying. "Slept badly last night." She wiped away black water from beneath her eyes with her thumb. "I'm sorry. Everything got too much. I felt bad about the garage and the break-in... all my crap affecting Wallace and his home... I was scared what might happen next. I feel so responsible."

"Which is why you left," he said in a matter of fact manner, handing her a white tissue out of a pack in his pocket.

"Yes." Indigo mopped up the water on her face.

"I've had a long chat with Wallace." He stroked her hair and kissed her head. "Earlier today. I had to go away for a few days with work. Sorry, Indigo. I should have been there. Are you all right now?"

"Yes. Just had a fright."

"I'll make us some tea. Come sit on the bed."

Indigo rubbed her cheek.

"Sorry about that." William looked tired. "You were hysterical and disorientated."

"Doesn't matter. Next time you snore, I'll get my own back."

William laughed a deep throaty sound that she hadn't heard for a while.

"I am sorry though, Indigo. I should have been in touch. Bloody demons got hold of me - and work. Should've known better."

"Finn's been round, and you know I met Wallace."

William nodded.

"How did you know I was here?"

"You weren't at the campsite so it was the obvious next choice - to me anyway."

"I suppose it was. Work's okay?"

"Yes, some investigating - private work. Can't talk about it yet as it's ongoing." He threw a couple of small logs in the burner. "You know it'll be Christmas in a few weeks. Wallace asked me to give you this." He handed her an envelope. "It's an invitation to the Bass Rock Golf Club annual Christmas bash - a horribly drunken affair that's good fun but takes days to recover from."

"Will you be going?"

William looked down for a moment.

"Aye, I was hoping we could go together. You'll have to wear a strip of my tartan even though you probably have your own."

"I'm happy to wear yours." Indigo took the bone china tea cup from William. The cup tap danced on the saucer. She was surprised at how much her hand was shaking. William steadied it with his large warm one.

"It's a Highland tartan of blue and green that I wear. The yellow MacLeod is a bit too loud and out there for me."

"You're a Highlander?"

"Aye, Clan MacLeod of Lewis." His eyes glittered as he sat down on the bed next to her. "How did your lunch with Finn go today?" He knew about the kiss. Bloody Finn, thought Indigo. Why did he have to tell William everything? She was right in her analysis that he was childlike.

"I made him monkfish. He seemed to like it. He's very creative, had some good ideas about the crazy golf - he told you about that?"

"Aye, and that he'd kissed you." William frowned. "My own fault for leaving a beautiful woman on her own at such a time."

Indigo didn't know how to respond. She stared down miserably at her tea, feeling the moist heat drifting to her nose.

"He apologised, said he'd always wanted to and couldn't stop himself - but that you hadn't kissed him back and you're still pals. He's very fond of you, as am I."

"You're not cross?" Indigo looked at him. Long dark lashes framed his bright eyes. His skin was smooth with just a trace of laughter lines around the eyes.

"No. As I said, it was my fault. Should have guessed how vulnerable you are right now."

"What about Finn? Are you annoyed with him?"

William smiled.

"He's like a brother to me. A bit. But I know he's bonkers. I told him not to worry about it but if he did it again he'd have me to deal with."

Indigo laughed and then saw that he was serious.

William was right, she was vulnerable and it annoyed her. Guilty thoughts whispered to her. 'See how understanding he is and you wanted Finn. You wanted to make love to him.' 'I'm only human,' she wanted to scream. Maybe she was sick of having to be strong all the time. It was exhausting.

"Well, I expect I encouraged him without realising," she responded weakly.

"Why don't you get into bed?" William smoothed her hair behind her ear. "I'll stay with you tonight if you don't mind, make sure you get a proper night's sleep."

Indigo nodded and went to clean her teeth. Standing in the tiny bathroom space that resembled an aeroplane toilet, she realised that William did mind about the kiss despite what he'd said. His eyes held an expression that she couldn't fathom. Was it resignation that all women would cheat on him or disappointment or anger? Maybe it was her own guilt projecting her emotions onto him. Tiredness engulfed her. She was sick of thinking.

Climbing into bed, she was surprised to see William stripping off his clothes. She'd imagined that due to their misunderstanding he'd sleep on cushions on the floor. His body was toned with not an ounce of spare flesh. Taking her firmly in his arms, his lips were insistent. He made love to her that night with a passionate dominance that had previously been absent. Hours later, she rested her head on his shoulder and fell into a deep sleep. The campervan creaked as the wind whipped around the bay, blowing an eerie low rhythm with rain, the percussion pattering on the roof, rocks and sand. William lay with his eyes open, listening to Indigo's regular breathing. His mind was troubled and he couldn't sleep.

TWELVE

A New Day

Indigo awoke the next morning feeling refreshed and fulfilled. She turned and gazed at William's sleeping profile. Unusual dark shadows rested beneath his eyes and a pallor affected his skin. There was something wrong. She had sensed it the night before but attributed it to the circumstances of his arrival and the knowledge of the kiss she had shared with Finn. William looked like a man who had not long succumbed to sleep. Therefore he was troubled. Indigo knew. She had experienced many broken nights and seen the ravages the next day in the mirror. Leaning over she kissed him lightly on the cheek. He meant so much to her. He was the first man she had ever admired. Despite her desire for Finn, she truly loved William.

Climbing out of bed, she was careful not to disturb him as she stacked the wood burner and lit kindling. Glancing out of the window at the early morning, the visibility was zero as their world was enveloped in sea mist, or 'the haar from the sea' as it is known on the east coast of Scotland. Grey sky mirrored the ocean offering no distinction between skyline and sea. It was as though a cloud had descended upon the Earth. It was the perfect ambience for murder to be committed. Mike should become better acquainted with the local weather and use it for his gain, she thought sourly.

A dull feeling hit her stomach as thoughts of Mike punctured her good mood. Glancing at William, her smile lifted her energy. Their love making had been exceptional. Full of passion and strength, William had brought her to the brink of pleasure, held her there and opened a world of indescribable sensation. It was as though they had become a joint energy, shimmering white and vibrating. Ecstatic pulses shot through her followed by waves of lightness and warmth, leaving her feeling loved, powerful and invincible. He was the best lover she'd ever had.

Brewing a cup of tea, she perched on the side of the bed gently stroking his hair. There was a large bump on his head. Parting the dark hair, she saw traces of blood and a stitched gash. William murmured in his sleep, moving his head away from her touch and grinding his teeth together as he muttered incoherently. As Indigo removed her hand, he suddenly grasped her arm in a vice-like grip. Breathing in, she silenced herself. For a second he squeezed her limb and then his fingers loosened and he returned to sleep.

Sitting cross-legged in front of the wood burner, she absorbed three meditations, silently repeating the invocations. Afterwards she took a shower and applied make-up, dressing in jeans, boots and a black jumper. Her mobile `phone was flashing. It was a message from her solicitor asking her to make an appointment to come in to the Edinburgh office to sign some papers. The purchase of Fisherman's Watch was going through. Excitement sent an array of butterflies to her belly. Switching on the kettle, she made tea for two. William stirred in his sleep. Stretching, he rubbed the back of his hand over his eyes.

"What time is it?" he asked groggily, half asleep.

"Eleven."

"What? I've got things to do..." He sat up, his face creased with bad temper.

"You needed sleep. Don't argue. I've made you some tea."

"Police don't do lateness - or excuses." He swung his legs out of bed. Black bruises covered his shoulders. She hadn't noticed them before due to the dim lighting.

"William," she breathed. "We need to talk." She eased her breath outwards to calm her racing pulse. Handing him the mug of tea, she continued. "You have new stiches on your head - which I think you did yourself - and bruises all over you. What the hell's going on?"

William took a sip of his tea and glared at her.

"Do I ask you everything about your life? Your Reiki? Your plans for Fisherman's Watch?" he snapped.

Indigo's stomach began to churn. A confrontation was the last thing she needed.

"I haven't seen you to tell you about anything. You didn't reply to my text."

"Some elements of life are private, Indigo. Like your plans, your liaison with Finn, your need to find yourself, etcetera. None of which include me. Then when I turn up covered in bloody bruises, I get the Spanish Inquisition."

"I was just concerned. William, that's a bit of an over-reaction..."

"I'm not some fanny, Indigo, that you need worry about." He swore violently and climbed out of bed, standing naked in front of her with his hands on his hips. "You should worry about yourself and your life. I'm more than capable of looking after myself. Ever thought of that? I don't want fixing!" he roared. They stood glaring at each other as he pulled on his clothes. Indigo swallowed, staring at him in astonishment. She felt sick.

"Then get the hell out." Indigo pointed to the door. "And don't bother coming back."

"Fine, I'll do that." As he reached for the door, Indigo clutched his arm.

"William, no!"

His eyes bore into hers and for a moment she thought he was going to push her out of the way, but then his expression softened.

"I'm acting like a prick."

"Drink your tea and then we'll talk. We've got enough to contend with without us fighting."

"Aye, you're right there." He sat on the floor in front of the merry blazing fire and Indigo handed him his tea. "You haven't said that I'm not acting like a prick?" He smiled.

"That's because you are, but I'm sure there's good reason." She stroked his face. "Bacon, eggs, sausage and potato cakes?"

"Now you're acting like an angel." He grinned. "I'm sorry. I over-reacted, you're right. Had a shit night's sleep, got too much on my mind."

"I thought you were on leave anyway? So you don't need to go in?"

William nodded and yawned widely, showing white even teeth.

"Was half asleep – aye, no rush to report in."

Indigo cooked breakfast while William sat staring into the flames. After they had eaten at the tiny table, Indigo refilled their tea mugs. The haar had lifted but rain fell in large droplets onto the roof. It was snug and warm inside the campervan.

"I was trying to protect you by not telling you what I've been up to. Don't want you worrying - but not telling you just causes more upset. You have a right to know."

"Know what? What's going on, William?"

"The night you went off to the campsite – well, I went too. Pitched a tent nearby." He looked down at his hands.

"Oh my God, William!"

"Only because of the situation with Mike, you understand. I was worried for your safety with that nutter about."

"Ah, so it was you rustling in the darkness?" Indigo felt relieved. "I was sure I spotted someone in the shadows, late - a few times when I glanced out of the window." Then confusion encompassed her. "The night of the fire... he had a cloak on! I never thought about it. Must have been the bash on the head."

William looked wary. For a moment they looked at each other in silence.

"I wasn't creeping about in the shadows. But there is a cloaked figure, you're right. Sounds bizarre!" He grimaced. "Wish it was a joking matter. It's not." He took a sip of tea. "This Mike, he's got a record for assault in the past on three women, one of whom accused him of rape but it didn't stand up in court due to lack of evidence."

"What?" Indigo felt her eggs and potato cakes threatening to return. Getting up, she put the kettle on and made another pot of tea.

"Yes. He's a nasty piece of work by all accounts. We tracked him to a rented cottage in the Borders. He's staying there with a woman, holidaying apparently. He's quite wealthy?"

Indigo nodded.

"Yes, loaded. Self-made business man."

"I spied a figure in a dark cloak milling around the campervan shortly after you'd arrived and photographed him setting off the firework. I didn't intervene because I need to gather evidence against him. This time the evidence has to be airtight, Indigo. The guy's a piece of shit."

Indigo poured hot, steaming brown tea into mugs, adding a dash of milk.

"Ta. Lovely breakfast. Feel less grouchy." He pulled her to him as she went to remove his plate. Kissing her gently, he ran his hands over her breasts and buttocks. "You're so sexy."

Indigo raised her eyebrows.

"Can we finish the horror story first? Discovering that my ex is a complete psycho doesn't quite do it for me." She pulled a face at William. He twisted his mouth and released her.

"Hmm.... aye, fair point!" He took a gulp of tea. "I filmed him the next night creating the ring of fire around the van. As soon as it was lit he crept away back to his jeep which he'd left up on the road. I'd purposely hid behind a caravan en route and as he sneaked past I jumped him - to get proof of identity. I'd already taken a pic of the vehicle to prove he was in the vicinity at that time, but needed a facial shot."

"I take it things didn't go well."

"No. I tripped him as he scuttled past and he went over. His face was covered by a black balaclava, which I hadn't expected. He's a vicious bugger - went for me and we rolled around punching and kicking, with me trying to pull of the mask... Definitely male, about my height though stockier."

Indigo's eyes widened.

"Not Findlay." William shook his head. "Finn's taller and fights like a girl. I know. We've had thousands of punch-ups since we were kids."

"That's a relief!"

"Is it though? Finn, I could have given a good hiding to and sent back to the monks, but this fella's a different matter."

"That's how you got the bruises?"

"Aye. He fared worse... but he's tough, fit for an old boy."

"Don't be catty."

William grinned.

"I gave him a good few hefty punches and pinned him to the ground. Was just about to rip that damn balaclava off when he booted me in the back with his heel and whacked me over the head with a rock. I think he would have tried to finish me but the old fella in the trailer opposite you appeared with his dog and he ran off."

"William, he could have killed you!"

"No. I would have prevented it. Just stunned me for a second. Never would have happened ten years ago - must be getting old." He smiled. "Felt like I mucked up our one chance to nail him, Indigo - hence my bad temper."

Indigo felt sickened. Mike had always been an aggressive bully. He'd beaten her up in the past but she'd had no idea he was capable of this or the other assaults.

"By the time I got to the road, he'd gone. Must have driven at speed. Radioed the car through to the station but was too late. The jeep was parked outside his cottage when the police arrived and his girlfriend gave him an alibi." He put his mug in the sink. "When questioned about the photo of his jeep on the road near the campsite he said he stopped for a moment on his way back from Edinburgh to check the route, and she said she was with him."

"What about the bruises? He must have had some?"

"Said it was up to them what they got up to in the bedroom and suggested my colleagues try S & M."

"Nice! Yuck, he's revolting." She laughed scornfully. "This is not good."

"No. Now he knows I'm on the case he'll go to ground for a while. Expect a lull and then he'll try to catch us unawares."

"So although the jeep is linked to Mike and he's staying in the Borders, we can't prove he's the cloaked figure?"

"He's saying that you wrecked his home out of spite because he dumped you for Catherine Thompson from Whitstable."

"He's a liar! She's welcome to him," Indigo spluttered furiously. "What do we do now?"

"Go back to bed?" William touched his head. "And I'd feel happier if you at least parked the campervan next to my cabin, Indigo, just to be on the safe side. Now we know what we're dealing with."

"I agree." She poked the fire with an iron. "I'm sorry about everything, William."

"Hardly your fault."

"I had no idea about him - his past. Maybe it is my fault. If I hadn't wrecked his house..."

"He'd have come after you anyway. It's the rejection. You leaving, he can't deal with, and the fact you stood up to him. Seems you got off lightly compared to his ex. He hospitalised her.

Fortunately she's okay now but was lucky to live. Again there was lack of evidence to put him away - her word against his."

Indigo shuddered as icy claws crept down her spine.

"What happens if he carries on with this vendetta and we can't get the evidence to send him down or stop him? Will this just go on and on?" She put her head in her hands.

William shook his head.

"We have a contingency plan."

Indigo looked up in surprise.

"Finn will drop him off the edge of a cliff. He says everyone thinks he's mental anyway."

"Don't joke. I'm serious! What will happen?"

William smiled with his mouth but his eyes were serious.

"Not sure. We'll have to see." He glanced out of the window at a dog walker. "People go walking in all weathers for their dogs and health. You know, I saw a man the other night when I was on duty - pitch black it was - he was wandering along the cliff paths completely unaware of the dangers lurking - loose bricks in barrier walls, crumbling earth and slate, natural gouges out of the cliff that aren't fenced off. You know, a poor wee dog nearly fell to its death the other week. Surprised there haven't been more fatalities."

"William, that's enough!" Indigo felt close to tears. "You can't kill him, he's not worth it."

"Sorry, but I won't stand by and see him destroy you. Everything'll be fine, you'll see." He kissed her forehead.

"Shall we clear up and drive to your place?" said Indigo.

William nodded.

"We'll pop in and see how Finn's getting on with the sketches."

◆ ◆ ◆

The next few weeks proved uneventful, as William had predicted. Indigo moved back into the cabin and immersed herself in her spiritual routine. The survey for Fisherman's Watch echoed her findings. The roof needed replacing and there was mild dry rot and a woodworm infestation. Other than that, she could concentrate on refurbishment. The house sale was moving fast and nearing completion due to the fact that there was no chain. Life became enjoyable and calm, despite the threat of Mike hanging over them.

William's colleague questioned Mike again regarding his whereabouts on the night of the ring of fire. The officer accused him of harassing Indigo, using the black cloak to terrify her. Mike just laughed, denying the charges.

"He's saying you're making it up to ruin his life," William told Indigo. "Says you're unstable, into witchcraft, and it's always been a fantasy of yours to have sex with a proper wizard - that's where you got the idea of the cloaked figure from."

"What the... that's more than bizarre!"

"When my colleague told him that another person had witnessed the cloak – me - he said we were in it together, trying to discredit him."

Resentment at his lies exploded within her. Mike had hampered her spiritual development, her healing process and her new life. Without his vendetta she would have progressed naturally and moved forward by now. However, maybe the higher powers needed her to experience this, to become stronger and develop resilience. If this was the case, then she had passed the test. She had never felt so strong, confident and capable.

THIRTEEN

The Ball

The evening of the Golf Club Christmas Ball arrived. Snow fell. Huge frosted flakes of purity drifted silently to the earth, coating the frozen ground with a soft illuminated peace. Indigo applied her make-up with care, adding eyeliner to her brown shimmering lids and waterline before adding a third layer of mascara. A subtle red kissed her lips. Powdering her nose, she glanced at William who was standing in full Scottish dress staring out of the bedroom window at the loch. He wore the MacLeod of Lewis tartan of checked blues with a smattering of moss green cubes. He looked stunningly handsome, but twitchy. Draining his whisky, he turned and watched her tong her long dark hair into soft waves.

"You look beautiful," he said simply. Walking up behind her, he kissed the crown of her head.

"So do you." She fiddled with her hair. "But tense - what's the matter?"

"Just feel a bit uptight... bit uncomfortable."

"Kilt too tight?" Indigo smiled. "Put on a few pounds since you last wore it?"

William laughed.

"Just got this feeling of foreboding." He moved his hand to his stomach. "Feel funny about tonight for some reason. Mike's been too quiet - makes me feel uneasy."

"What time are your parents arriving?"

"Got a text from my Dad last night. They're coming back after Christmas now. Sorry, I thought I said." He massaged her shoulders. "Wish we could stay home."

Indigo gently removed his hand from her shoulder.

"I need to dress or we'll be late."

William sighed.

"Is this your overnight bag?" He pointed to Indigo's suitcase. "It'll just be one night in the campervan at the golf club, won't it?"

"No." Indigo looked puzzled. "Don't you remember? We agreed to spend a few nights in the van up near Fisherman's Watch. Or weren't you listening?"

"We have a perfectly good warm house here, Indigo."

"Keeps me grounded. I just fancy a change. Want to be up near the house so I can make plans for the renovation."

"Okay." He shook his head. "We'll camp out in the middle of a Scottish winter. Could be a survival challenge, aye. Completely bonkers you are. I'll pack half my wardrobe too then, shall I?"

Indigo laughed.

"You're fine about your parents not coming home?"

"Aye, too cold for my mother. Apparently her bad knee's been playing up and the damp cold here will aggravate it further. They should see about renting out the house - seems a waste. My mother's funny about other people living there though, even me. What did your solicitor say about a completion date for Fisherman's Watch?"

"Mid to end of January, which is why I've put the kids off coming to stay until Easter. They'll stay with their grandparents in France for Christmas. The plan is that they'll move into Fisherman's Watch after uni. They're so excited about the house, bless them."

"The Scottish air will see them right after cramming for exams. Why are they in the same year?"

"Lily took a year out. She spent a year travelling."

"Good for her. You'll be okay with Ella tonight? You know she's accompanying Finn?"

"Yes, he said." Indigo looked at him innocently. Secretly she was dreading seeing Ella.

"You're not jealous?" William narrowed his eyes.

"Oh, shut up!" Indigo threw a cushion from the bed at him. "*He* kissed *me*, you know that."

"Don't let him next time. It's as simple as that." He pulled her up from the bed, kissing her lightly.

142

"Get me a glass of wine while I finish dressing, would you?"

◆ ◆ ◆

Indigo and William stood in the red carpeted reception area of the golf club before being ushered into the ballroom. Indigo was pleased with her appearance. Her make-up and hair enhanced her natural good looks and she wore an elegant, long black sleeveless dress that clung to her slender figure with William's tartan sash draped around the hips. Black stilettoes hugged her feet. Finn came over at once to greet them. He looked striking in full dress with a dark blue and green kilt. Embracing them, he grabbed champagne from a passing waiter's tray and thrust glasses at them.

"You'll need this. Ella's already pissed!" He raised his eyes to Heaven.

The subtly lit room was large with a mahogany bar that curved around one side, laden with optics and gleaming glasses. White-clothed tables sat at intervals around a shiny wooden dance floor. A vast Christmas tree stood in splendour at the far end of the room, adorned with colourful lights and red and gold baubles. Candles burned in ornate Christmas tea light holders and the smell of festive roast dinner wafted around the room, mingling with a multitude of perfumes and aftershaves.

"We're over here." Finn pointed to a round table at which Wallace was seating with a pretty woman of about sixty-five, dressed in a midnight blue velvet dress. Her silver hair was pinned up and diamonds hung sparkling from her earlobes. She must be the long-term lover from Dirleton, Indigo thought. Ella sat on his right. Indigo tried to ignore the twinge of hatred she felt towards her. Ella was a disturbed soul to be pitied more than hated. Ella drained her glass of champagne as they approached and refilled it from the silver ice bucket on the table.

Wallace stood up and kissed Indigo.

"You look lovely, my dear." He introduced his date as 'a good friend'. "This is Paula, a dear friend of mine."

The woman smiled. She had large brown twinkly eyes and Indigo immediately warmed to her.

They shook hands.

"And of course you know Ella." He sat back down.

Indigo smiled weakly at Ella who looked beautiful in green velvet. Her hair was up and tendrils trickled down her neck. Her sea green eyes were warmer than usual due to the amount of alcohol consumed. Her eyes travelled from Indigo to William and tension built around the table for a moment. Reverting to Indigo she smiled warmly.

"We haven't been formally introduced," she spoke softly. "I'm Ella - you probably know me better as drunken jealous bitch."

Indigo raised her eyebrows and with effort took the proffered hand with a firm grip. How she would love to respond, 'Yes I do', and tip champagne over her perfect hair. But it would embarrass Wallace in front of his golfing cronies so she refrained and said instead:

"I'm Indigo, or tree-hugging witch who should be drowned or burned at the stake." Smiling innocently, she watched with amusement as surprise registered on Ella's face. Scottish folk music began to pulse throughout the room at a deafening level before the volume was rapidly reduced. Elderly folk around the room spluttered with outrage, adjusting hearing aids and calling waiters over to complain.

Ella narrowed her eyes for a moment and then threw back her head and laughed.

"Finn insists I apologise or he won't spank me later. I'm sorry about the spiteful letters. I don't know what to say – sorry, I shouldn't have done it. Merry Christmas." She raised a glass.

"Apology accepted." Lying, Indigo clinked her glass to Ella's. Despite the apology she still felt animosity towards the woman. Ella glanced at William who was staring at her intently.

"Looking devastatingly handsome as usual, cuz." She was seated next to Finn and Indigo sat on his left with William by her side next to Paula. William whispered in Indigo's ear.

"You're a terrible liar, but I'm the only one who knows." He kissed her earlobe and filled their glasses with champagne.

Finn smiled into her eyes.

"Dance with me later, Indigo?"

"Of course." It suddenly occurred to Indigo that she didn't know any Scottish dances. "As long as it's a simple dance."

"We'll dance a slow one," he grinned.

The chairman of the golf club gave a welcoming speech. The

dancing would open with a display by local dancers. William and Finn left their seats and joined four other men of a similar age on the dance floor. The chairman handed out six swords and the men placed them on the wooden floor, each dancer standing behind his sword. A bagpiper appeared and began to play.

"Male Highland Sword Dance," said Wallace. "Unfortunately my hip's not up to it these days - very energetic."

Indigo watched as the six men elegantly bounced effortlessly around and over their swords with arms up and footwork worthy of ballerinos. The motion flung their kilts from side to side displaying glimpses of muscular bare thighs. They danced in perfect unison, leaping from one side of the sword to the other. It was a rhythmic dance, perfectly executed and sexy. As the beat quickened, the footwork became more intricate, pulsing energy into the room. It was an impressive display. The men returned to the table grinning and glistening with sweat. Loud applauses echoed. The waiter brought over beers from the bar. Finn slumped down next to Indigo.

"I'm knackered."

"I'm impressed!"

William drank down a glass of water and kissed Indigo. She noticed that he was barely out of breath.

"Didn't know you could dance like that."

"Learned at High School. Enjoyed that." He sat down. "Starving!" He gulped down half of his pint.

"There's a carvery that'll be open shortly," said Wallace.

Indigo had the vegetarian alternative of roast potatoes, Yorkshire puddings, carrots, broccoli, cauliflower cheese and vegetarian gravy. The boys piled their plates up with turkey, stuffing, pigs in blankets and as many roast potatoes as they could fit on their plates. Ella returned with a small amount of turkey, vegetables and one roast potato.

"That wouldn't feed a sparrow," said Finn heartily, stuffing a whole potato into his mouth.

Ella grimaced.

"Your table manners are foul for someone who went to public school," she snapped nastily. "I'm going out for a fag." Stomping off, she left the plate of food untouched.

"Fowl indeed," grinned Finn, forking up some turkey.

"What's up with her?" asked William.

"Probably pissed off because the limelight isn't on her," said Finn, draining his pint and waving the waiter over for another.

"You two getting on okay?" asked William, refilling Indigo's glass with wine.

"Some of the time."

"You could've kept it casual, with her still in Yorkshire."

"Ella decides she wants something, she gets it." He sighed. "It has its compensations."

William grinned.

"Yeah, but is it worth the hassle?"

When the waiter had cleared the plates, couples took to the dance floor.

"May I borrow you beautiful girlfriend, William?" asked Finn.

William was fiddling with his mobile 'phone, frowning.

"Aye, go ahead," he said absentmindedly.

Finn led Indigo to the dance floor. Taking her into his arms he held her closely so her cheek was pressed to the hard wall of his chest. A hint of frankincense, ginger and sandalwood wafted to her nostrils.

"I don't wear anything under my kilt," he whispered softly. "If you don't believe me..."

Indigo laughed.

"Findlay, what would William say? You've already told him about the kiss. Were you trying to break us up?" She looked up into his merry blue eyes.

Finn looked startled.

"No! God knows I'm not like that. I kissed you. He's my best mate. I told him because at the time I felt it was the right thing to do, so he'd know it was me that instigated it and you wouldn't feel bad."

"Oh, okay. I believe you."

"Will you stay with him?"

"Yes. I think the world of you Finn, but I love him."

"We could have an affair, you and I." He breathed in the scent of her hair. "They don't need to know."

"But we would, Finn. I'm not going to lie. We both know there's chemistry between us but I don't want to live like that, sneaking around, having affairs, complicating my life. It would only bring heartache in the end. I want to be respectable and settle down and I've finally met someone I respect and love.

Never had that before."

"You could have that with me. I'm here if you ever change your mind. We'll be good pals, shall we?"

"Sure." She smiled up at him and he kissed her softly on the mouth. Indigo felt her arm being pulled as Ella literally yanked her away from Finn's grasp. William appeared between them.

"That's not helping, mate, is it?" he said sternly to Finn. "That's twice now. I won't stand for it again."

"We were just talking - sealing our platonic friendship. Nothing more to it." Finn's eyes glittered with mischief.

"Your girlfriend's making a play for my man." Ella went for Indigo who moved quickly away.

"We're just friends," Indigo spoke calmly. Ella was drunk and out of control. She felt like screaming at her about her past behaviour and the threatening letters.

"Aye, looked that way." Ella glared at her.

"You've a cheek after what you've done," Indigo snapped crossly, returning to the table. Pouring a glass of wine, she drained half of it. How she hated her.

If it hadn't been for William she would have grabbed Finn and kissed him in front of Ella just to spite her. Really, she must ground herself; negativity was oozing from every pore of her being. Rebecca would say that she was leaking energy like a slow puncture. Ella, like Mike, had the uncanny ability to upset her.

Finn ignored Ella. Turning, he stalked off to the bar leaving William to defuse the situation. Ella was unstable and should be locked up. William was dancing with her, trying to placate her. Taking a deep breath, Indigo silently performed some grounding and protection exercises. Immediately she felt her energy increase and waves of serenity encompass her. Finn returned with a bottle of whisky and champagne.

"Sorry, Indigo." He sat down next to her. "I should think before I act. Ever since the accident, I just seem to react without considering the consequences. Gone back to Freud's id stage: 'I am therefore I want'. And it seems I want instant gratification. Doctor says it could take years to return to normal..."

"I doubt you were normal to start with." Indigo smiled fondly at him. "She's a handful, Finn."

"I know, but she has a lovable side too. Not sure if the bad outweighs the good these days though. I'll have to see. How are things with you now? All that trouble with your ex cleared up?"

"He's been quiet. William's twitchy about it."

"Understandably." He sipped his whisky. "Sorry I kissed you again – it was an impulse."

"Finn, we have chemistry and probably always will. You fancy me and I you, but we both have to ignore it. We're with other people." Indigo fiddled with her champagne glass. "Otherwise it's gonna make our friendship difficult and I don't want to lose that. I value what we have."

"Me too." He looked at William dancing with Ella. "I know about them. The past, when we were kids. They think I don't. I read Ella's diaries. I'm an artist and therefore inquisitive."

"Bullshit! Damn right nosey more like!"

Finn laughed.

"Yeah, okay. Don't have those kinda scruples, no."

"I would've, too, if I'd come across William's diary. I know we're supposed to be above that kind of thing but I'd've been curious too."

The folk music began and they watched William and Ella dance the Gay Gordon.

"She seems to have cheered up." 'Silly bitch,' thought Indigo, watching Ella laughing as she moved gracefully on the dance floor.

"She has male attention," said Finn. "Are you going to dance? Duke of Perth is a mild dance."

"Might as well make a fool of myself."

The dancing was becoming wilder as champagne and whisky flowed. People whooped, reeling around the dance floor arm in arm. Indigo took to the floor with Finn as William disappeared out into reception with his `phone.

Taking Finn's hands she spun around before linking arms with a new partner, then another. Indigo was trying to co-ordinate but had to rely on the generosity of the other dancers to help her. Dodging in an out, she skipped around the floor, spun from one gentleman to another. Round and round, her dark hair fanned out in the breeze clutching the veined ice-cold hands of an elderly man with bushy white eyebrows. Then she danced with a young man who stared at her cleavage the whole time and then one of Wallace's golfing partners who shouted to her in an attempt at conversation but she couldn't hear him. All too soon the dance was over and they sat down. Indigo was short of breath.

"That was fun!" she gasped.

"You're a natural dancer." Finn took a drink of beer. "If you like Scottish dancing I can teach you some more. There'll be other events and it'll be fun for you to learn."

"Sure Ella would love that!"

"Stuff Ella." Finn was looking around the room.

"Think she went outside."

"I was actually wondering where William's got to." He picked up his `phone and checked his messages. "Won't be a minute." He disappeared out to reception. Wallace and Paula were dancing and Indigo felt stupid sitting at the table alone, so followed Finn out. He and William were standing in reception engrossed in an intense discussion. Indigo stopped for a moment admiring the two men, both so handsome and distinguished. William immediately looked over and smiled.

"You look flushed. Been having fun?"

"Yes, great fun actually. Been dancing." She walked over. "What are you two up to?"

"Oh, nothing." His face held a dark tension.

"William!" Indigo suddenly felt scared. "Mike?"

"He's only been sighted in the area. I'd asked my colleagues to keep an eye out. They followed him for a bit but got a call out to one of the pubs and had to attend. Lost him after that." He put his arm around her and hugged her. "Try not to worry."

"Easier said... Where's Ella?" Indigo asked.

"Chatting up one of Wallace's wealthy widower friends. They're smoking and guzzling champagne in the conservatory with the patio door open. They're both so pissed they think no-one knows they're smoking. Good mind to issue them with a fine."

"Nice," said Finn. "Bored of me already."

"She's just getting back at you for flirting with me, that's all," reassured Indigo.

Finn looked disgruntled.

"Bored of stupid games. Want to meet a nice girl like you, Indigo. Do you have any sisters?" he added quickly, seeing William's cross expression.

"Only me, I'm afraid!"

William's `phone rang.

"It's the station, I better get it." His face fell and then darkened with fury. Ending the call, he swore violently and kicked the leather sofa.

"William, what the hell's the matter?" cried Indigo.

William's intense eyes were full of primitive rage. A murderous expression masked his handsome face. Indigo suddenly got a flash of a different side to him. A distant, ruthless dimension. He was so angry it took a moment for him to calm down enough to speak.

"Bastard's set fire to the cabin. Burned it to the ground. Fire brigade's there now but too late to save it."

Indigo head began to spin and she felt the two men catch her, laying her on the brown leather sofa. It took a moment for the shock to subside before clarity returned. William's home and possessions had been destroyed.

"I'll rip his head off! Don't ask me to go gently now, Indigo," snarled William through gritted teeth. "He's gonna get what's coming to him. He made the choice to start this - now he'll have to face the consequence of his actions."

Finn agreed.

"Too bloody right, mate."

Indigo's energy plummeted to the floor as fear swarmed through her. The sense that someone's life was in peril was so strong it was suffocating. War had been declared and there was nothing she could do to prevent the bloodshed that was to follow.

FOURTEEN

William's colleagues drove them in a marked police car to the site of the smouldering cabin. The dark landscape of the early hours was embroidered with sparkling white pearls as a steady trickle of glistening ice droplets poured from the thick mauve clouds. Driving past the loch, a pile of black and charred, sodden firewood sat in place of William's former home. Indigo heard his sharp intake of breath as they stood viewing the sordid scene. The stench of burning rubber and charcoal hung in the air. Stumps of burnt trees, fellow victims of the arsonist, added to the macabre scene as fire greedily devoured part of the small surrounding forest. Wisps of black smoke rose from the ashes. A black-stained Victorian bathroom suite stood exposed to the elements and burned-out kitchen white goods, vandalised beyond redemption, looked sadly on. Indigo daren't look at William, who was in deep conversation with the firemen who had extinguished the fire. William walked over to her, still in full Scottish dress.

"A neighbour walking his dog saw the blaze and called the brigade. Definitely arson. Colin from the station will drive us up to Fisherman's Watch." He sighed. "My other colleague Jim'll take the campervan up to the field as we've been drinking." He ran his fingers through his hair. "Too hot to retrieve anything." He nodded towards the cabin. "But it'll soon cool in these temperatures. Better in daylight."

"William..."

He glanced at her. His expression was dark and he looked

tired. The air was freezing with a bitter wind chill. Indigo shivered despite her white fake fur jacket.

"I can't talk about this right now..." His eyes watered and he looked down at his 'phone.

"You should go sit in the car." He wiped his eyes with the palm of his hand. "Eyes're streaming - smoke and this bloody ferocious wind. Cuts you in half! Need to call Finn." He disguised his upset well but Indigo knew he was devastated.

"Findlay, come with Jim to the campervan. Ella can go back with Wallace - and bring some serious booze." He paused. "Couldn't give a shit if she doesn't want to. Tell her!" he snarled, his face full of ill temper. Ending the call he stroked Indigo's hair absentmindedly. His fingers smelled of smoke. "Good job you insisted we stay in the van. I packed my laptop and iPad. And at least I have a change of clothes."

"I'm so sorry." Guilt consumed her. "If you'd never met me..."

"Don't start a guilt trip now. That'll just annoy me."

"But - "

"It's Mike who's responsible for this, not you. End of."

"I know, but - "

"Indigo. Drop it!" he snapped. To add insult, his kilt blew up in the wind on their way back to the car but the situation was too grave for her to laugh. Nature has no sense of occasion, she thought. Climbing into the police car, they drove up to Fisherman's Watch where Jim and Finn were waiting for them.

"Farmer okay with the van parked here, is he?" Jim addressed Indigo.

"Yes, I cleared it with him last week. Could we have it at the far end near the gate to Fisherman's Watch?" She pointed down the field. "Next to the remnants of the old bonfire - just over there."

"Aye." The policeman drove the van to the spot.

"Fairly sheltered here from the wind." Climbing out of the van he looked doubtfully up at the sky. "Not from the white stuff though. William, the wife and I could put you all up. You'll no want to be camping out in this. If we can help...?"

"We'll be all right here for a bit. The campervan has a wood burner. Best under the circumstances, I think. Thanks though, Jim, appreciate it."

Indigo felt another twinge of guilt. In other words, he didn't want Jim's home being destroyed by his girlfriend's psychotic pyromaniac arsonist ex-boyfriend. She kept her thoughts to herself.

"Aye, well, a patrol car will drive past and Colin's dropping your van off tomorrow."

"My bike's parked near the van. Is it possible to bring that too?" asked Indigo quietly. The policeman nodded and the two men shook hands gravely. Jim went with Colin back to the police station.

Indigo lit the wood burner and soon heat and light flickered and danced around the interior of the van, casting strange shapes upon the walls. Indigo squeezed into the tiny bathroom and awkwardly changed into her fleece pyjamas and thick thermal socks. Her feet were painfully cold after standing outdoors in minus nine degrees in a ball gown and stilettoes. Bloody Mike. It had been such an enjoyable evening. She couldn't even bear to think about the destruction to William's property. A dull sickness lay in the pit of her stomach. Returning to the lounge area, William and Finn were sitting at the small table drinking whisky and eating pork sandwiches, discussing the events of the evening.

"Indigo?" William gestured to the bottle of whisky.

"No, ta. I'm going to have a cup of tea and go to bed, but you two carry on. I'm tired." Filling a cup with green tea she poured the rest of the kettle into a hot water bottle. She climbed into bed and sleep took her to a world full of peace and calm.

◆ ◆ ◆

Awaking the next morning, she was surprised to see it was eleven o'clock. Having slept eight hours, her head felt clear despite the alcohol consumed at the ball. She attributed this to the large Christmas dinner she'd enjoyed and the crisp air of the early hours of the morning. Squashed up against the wall, she wriggled into a sitting position. William lay next to her sleeping deeply with his mouth open, dressed only in his kilt and tartan socks. Finn slept peacefully at the other end of the bed, hugging William's foot to his chest. He too wore his kilt with one of William's navy blue fisherman's sweaters.

Grinning, Indigo took a couple of pictures and a short video with her `phone. Hopefully in happier times ahead they could laugh at the sight. Two gorgeous men in her bed, she smiled, what a lucky girl. Clumsily, she clambered over the array of bodies trying not to wake them. Judging by the empty whisky bottle on the table they had not long fallen into bed.

She pulled back the curtain and brilliant light greeted her. The sun's rays illuminated the snowy iced landscape and the navy ocean heaved back and forth rhythmically, motoring vast frothing waves up the beach at speed. Gusts of wind shook the campervan intermittently. The police had brought William's van and her bike up as promised. Switching on the kettle, she relit the wood burner, relishing the heat from the fire. Her `phone bleeped. It was a text from one of the builders contacted with regard to the refurbishment project. North Berwick Contractors were delighted that she'd accepted their quote to do the building works. Would she contact them as soon as the sale was completed? Indigo took out her 'Things to do' list and wrote their name and number next to the proposed completion date. The relevant papers had been signed and the process was underway. Her house sale in Kent was nearing completion. Upon the sale and purchase being finalised, the builders would rebuild the roof and begin the renovations. Perhaps they could rebuild William's home in the meantime. Damn Mike for the pain he caused. A sick weight pressed against her solar plexus.

Clutching a mug of green tea with lemon, she put on headphones and concentrated on meditation. Tension oozed from her body, replaced by pulses of mauve energy lifting and motivating her mood. She called Reiki and spent ten minutes clearing her chakras. Feeling calm and energised, Indigo was now strong and capable despite Mike's evil actions.

Six eggs sat alone in the fridge. Bacon and sausages were needed for breakfast. There was only a thin covering of snow on the ground so it shouldn't be too icy to cycle down to the town for supplies. Moments later, dressed in Wellingtons, a thick lilac waterproof padded jacket over jeans and jumper, gloves, hat and scarf, she tore down to the shops. The piercing shriek of seagulls accompanied the hoarse howling of the wind and the throbbing of the breakers crashing against the coal crag. The gusts were stronger than anticipated, pushing her towards a ditch that ran alongside the country lane. Wobbling, she cursed the elements.

The sound of a diesel motor to her rear prompted her to slow. It sounded like a police car or taxi. The vehicle reduced speed and drew up alongside her. As she glanced to her right, the door on the passenger side suddenly swung open, knocking her off the bike into the shallow ditch. A pain shot through her arm as she hit the frozen ground. Before she could move, a black pillow case was thrust over her head. Screaming, she felt a dull thud to the side of her face.

"Shut up or I'll knock you out!"

She recognised Mike's voice immediately, well-spoken with the trace of a north England accent. Dragging her struggling body to the car, he lifted her crying onto the back seat. Indigo wriggled manically as he bound her hands behind her back and her legs at the knees and ankles, but he easily overpowered her.

"Lie there, shut up and keep still or I'll throttle you," he whispered menacingly, pressing his thumb onto her larynx. "I could, you know. I have total power over you."

Steel fear clamped her neck. Shock ricocheted through her. Stupidly, even now she still couldn't believe that Mike was capable of this.

"Why are you doing this?" she muttered.

She felt his hand underneath her coat, caressing her body in an attempt to humiliate her. She was in peril. Indigo began to pray to all seven archangels, Jesus and the universe for divine intervention. She would need it if she were going to escape from Mike unscathed.

"Because I can. And I said shut up, didn't I?" he growled. Slamming the door shut, he climbed back into the driver's seat. "See all the trouble you've caused me, babe? Can't have you back now you've been shagged by another man. You always were a stupid tart. You'll be punished for it, though, and for wrecking my house. Got another bird now, anyway. She does as she's told. Well, she has to," he laughed, slightly hysterically. "Your boyfriend's been causing me problems. This business would have been dealt with a while ago if it hadn't been for him poking his nose in." He braked suddenly, flinging Indigo off the seat onto the floor. "Yes, just you to deal with and then I'm off. Got a new life planned - just need a bit of closure…"

Pulling over to the side of the road, he opened the back door and rummaged inside Indigo's coat until he found her debit card.

"I want my housekeeping money back and payment for damages. Co-operate and I might let you live. What's your PIN?"

Indigo began to shake and muttered her four digit number. Increasing her prayers, she picked at the rope around her wrists trying to loosen it. The secret was to find the loosest loop and work on that first. They were all tight. Locking the car, Mike went to the cash point, returning moments later and putting the card back in her pocket. He sat back in the driver's seat.

"Not much in your account, Indigo. You always were such a loser. I took what's due to me – a hundred pounds housekeeping that you stole and four hundred damages for trashing the house. Leaves you with fifty. Although you won't need it," he chuckled. "I expect you thought you could treat me like shit and walk away. You bloody women. Speak to me!" he demanded.

"You told me to shut up!" Although she didn't want to antagonise him, she was aware that he already had her fate sealed in his mind.

"Well, now I'm telling you to speak, you stupid tart." His tone was brutal.

"Why did I treat you badly, Mike? `Cause I left you? You hurt me badly, the day you beat me up. Surely that's revenge enough?" Her voice was muffled inside the pillowcase, which smelled of cheap perfume.

"I just gave you a slap. Don't exaggerate. If it hadn't been for that damn cat you'd have been taught a lesson and would still be with me now instead of running off to Scotland with pretty boy."

Indigo couldn't stop shaking. There was no reasoning with him. She was freezing cold and terrified. Her teeth chattered as her senses rocketed to high alert. Calling on the angels for intervention, she remained quiet. As they hit the motorway, Mike put on the CD player and began to sing along to country and western songs. Psychopathic, he had no sense of conscience and seemed genuinely to believe that he was the victim and entirely blameless. The car bumped down a track and came to a halt. Indigo could hear the faint roll of the tide beating the cliffs in the distance. They must be about a mile from the sea. Mike's `phone rang.

"But I thought you were going to be away the night?" He sounded annoyed. "Cancelled...? You don't fancy staying... okay, no, okay... see you shortly. Byeee." He swore and opened the back door, pulling Indigo out and forcing her to stand against the car. "My new bird's gonna be home soon. If you make a sound or try to alert her, it's gonna be bad for you - and her. You understand? Her life is in your hands!"

He pulled the pillowcase and hat from her head. Indigo looked into his blue eyes. He looked the same as the last time she'd seen him, handsome with short brown hair but slimmer around the face. He'd parked in front of a small, remote stone cottage immersed within farmland. The sea was a mere smear of blue in the distance. His mouth found hers. Kissing her thoroughly, she could feel him hard against her. Bile rose from her stomach. His mouth tasted of stale coffee. Lime musk aftershave filled her nostrils. Yanking her hair back, he glared at her.

"Kiss me back." He pushed his tongue into her mouth. The sound of a tractor chugging up the lane interrupted his ardour and he let go of her. His eyes travelled over her face.

"Looking rough, Indigo. Doubt the boyfriend'll stay interested long. Man like that'll get a better looking, younger model. I'll be doing you a favour, saving you from all that heartache. He's just using ya for sex. You're an easy lay." He took out a penknife; Indigo felt dizzy with terror. Was he going to stab her here with a tractor approaching? Her legs lost power and she felt light-headed. But he simply cut the rope that bound her ankles and knees and propelled her towards the lonely farm cottage.

"Your room's in the cellar," he laughed. "Freezing cold, with spiders and pitch black at night. I know how much you love the dark!" He pushed her into the tiny house that was dimly lit with old, patterned beige wallpaper. A musty smell greeted them. Plunging his hands into her pockets, he removed her purse, `phone, scarf and gloves. As he opened the door to the cellar, coldness hit her and the stench of rotting vegetation and damp made her stomach churn. Pushed down the stairs, she fell onto the filthy floor, grateful for the cushion of her padded jacket. "Remember, you make a sound - I'll kill her and then you. I mean it. Tomorrow morning I'll come visit and we can play."

He slammed the door and she heard him lock and bolt it. Scrambling onto her knees, she managed to stand up. The cellar was not in total darkness; she could make out the outline of the walls. Again she called to the archangels for assistance. Mike had been sure he would have a night alone with Indigo. He had been genuinely surprised by the 'phone call from Catherine regarding the cancellation of her business and her imminent return. Indigo was certain that the angels were helping her.

"Please, archangels," she begged, sobbing and glancing in fright around the fug of blackness. A pulse of light shone on the wall opposite. A mere dot and then it vanished. Walking nearer, Indigo saw a narrow rectangular window at shoulder height, camouflaged by grimy glass and boarded up from the outside. Bending her neck to the side, she estimated that she could just get her head through the space. She was very slim and certain that the rest of her body would follow. But the immediate challenge was to rid her wrists of the rope.

The enormity of her situation hit her. Petrified, her breathing was shallow and sickness consumed her. She needed to calm down. Taking control of her breath, she sucked air down into her belly, held it there and slowly released it until her pulse regulated.

"Help me, please... Get me away from him... I need your protection and intervention," she whispered.

The dark cellar began to close in on her. Her hatred of darkness had begun in childhood when constant vivid nightmares hounded her. Awaking unseeing into the thick blanket of night had only increased her terror as disorientation reigned. Night lights were wasteful and forbidden in her childhood home.

Her thoughts travelled to William. At fourteen, he had been beaten and locked in the freezing cellar of his home, shrouded in blackness all night long with only rats and insects and his thoughts for company. How many nights had he suffered this fate? Indigo felt hatred towards his father for inflicting such cruelty on a young boy. She hoped his parents would stay in Dubai. They held no interest for her.

The sound of a car pulling up outside was followed by the pitch of a female voice and the low rumble of a man's. Climbing the stairs, Indigo tried to hear what was being said. Mike was obviously aroused by the afternoon's activities and was insisting on making love to Catherine on the floor by the cellar door, obviously for Indigo's benefit. She shuddered as she listened to their gasps of pleasure. He was disgusting. The sounds brought renewed dread for the following morning. If she didn't manage to flee, he would force himself upon her. After he'd raped her, he would kill her or leave her in the cellar to perish. There was no way he would set her free.

Indigo suspected that the farm cottage was not the original house the couple had rented for holiday purposes. It was far too small and down-market for Mike's lavish tastes. What if she were left there and William couldn't find her? As panic spiralled, the light again pulsed on the far wall and a warm calmness filled her. At least, if she were murdered the angels would look after her; but she didn't want to suffer a violent death and certainly wasn't ready to die. The children, William, Finn and Fisherman's Watch came to mind. She had to be strong.

Sitting on the cellar steps, she called Reiki and absorbed the surges of heat and strength. Her jeans caught on the jagged edge of the concrete step that had crumbled through age. Excitement filled her. Moving the rope back and forth against the rough surface, she willed it to fray. After a while she rested and then started again until the fibres slowly began to unravel. Rubbing it again faster against the step, she felt it give. Her wrists were free.

She could just make out the outline of her hands in the dimness. It must be mid-afternoon by now, time to get started on the window. If only she could find some tool to help her... Moving around the cellar space, she peered closely at the walls and floor. It was empty apart from a pile of rubble in one corner.

A slamming noise sounded outside followed by laughter and then car doors opening and shutting. The engine started and the car pulled away. Indigo began to feel around the floor, trying not to think about rats or spiders. A piece of metal that felt rough with a crumbling surface came to her touch. It was the size of a large ruler and she imagined it was rusty. Grasping it, she smashed it against the filthy glass window with all her strength. Nothing happened. Pulling her sleeve down to protect her hand from the jagged metal, she drove it onto the glass. It chipped. Thinking of Mike, she attached the pane in a furious frenzy. It splintered and then smashed into pieces. Wood boarding was nailed beyond with hairline cracks of light filtering through.

She pushed at the wood but it remained securely in place. Inserting the metal between the stone of the house and the wood, she levered it like a wrench. Then she took off one Wellington and bashed it further into the gap until the metal bar was wedged tightly. Replacing her boot, she prayed for strength and pulled back on the bar with all her might. The second time, she felt the nails that held the boarding begin to give. Resting for a moment, she attacked it with every ounce of determination she possessed. The wood made a banging sound and came away from the stone wall.

Daylight beamed into the cellar, showing water-stained walls and the carcasses of dead rats and discarded traps. Indigo shuddered. She levered the board from the wall of the cottage until it fell away to the side. The window appeared to be on ground level. She cleared the broken glass away with the piece of orange, rusty metal then threw it outside. Taking off her jacket, she pushed it through the window onto the gravel.

Ignoring the filth and dead insects, including the remains of large spiders, Indigo shifted the pile of rubble from the corner to beneath the window, to provide a step. She climbed up the rockery of broken bricks and stone and was able to reach her arms through the window. Moving her head to the side, she squeezed it through the gap. Her elbows grated against the ragged wall as she pushed against the stone, pulling her body upwards.

Fields of long grass waved in the breeze. The air smelled of ice and cold and a smattering of snow covered the earth.

Gasping as her skin grazed against the window frame, she realised that she was stuck, unable to move back or forwards. She couldn't get her bust through the space. Wedged half-way to freedom, half-imprisoned, she hung there. She had read some-where that if you could get your head through a gap, then it was physically possible for the rest of the body to follow - or was that only applicable to cats? Indigo took a deep breath and prayed for strength. She would rather rip her figure to shreds and crush her bones to powder than be discovered in this state by Mike upon his return. Propelling her frame upwards, she ignored the pain in her chest. Roaring with anger and courage, her body moved through the space to freedom. Somehow she managed to wriggle her lower self out of the cellar, rolling over onto the grey drive to lie on her back gasping, giving herself a few seconds to recover.

Her body felt wet around the waist; putting her hand on her jumper, she saw blood. Superficial wounds, she wasn't bothered about. Climbing to her feet, she carefully put on her jacket and picked up the metal. Then she replaced the wooden boarding against the cellar window and booted it into place. At a glance, it looked normal.

Time was of the essence. Moving around to the back of the house, she peered through the kitchen window, her heart racing. On the kitchen table were her belongings. She smashed the glass panel of the back door, reached in and turned the key. Picking up the ˈphone she saw there was no signal. As she stuffed her possessions into her pockets, she heard the sound of a car approaching. Grabbing a bottle of water from a worktop, she left the house and closed the door behind her.

Indigo sprinted through the small gate at the bottom of the garden and disappeared into acres of farmland. Crouching near the hedgerows, she moved as quickly as physically possible towards thick woods in the distance. Judging by the decrease in temperature and increase in wind power, she knew she must be heading towards the ocean. She pulled her ˈphone out of her pocket and saw one bar of radio signal - not enough to make a call, but a text might send. Contacting William was the priority.

'Mike took me. Help. Near Borders.' She pressed Send as she jogged up the side of the field, her breath coming out in gasps. Her body felt battered and exhausted but she didn't care. Escape had been achieved but now she had to ensure that he didn't find her. She wouldn't get a second chance. Glancing down at her text messages she saw a red 'X' next to the message to William - the message had failed to send. Damn it! She cursed and began to run. A stile loomed ahead. It was the only way forward. Keeping as low as possible, she scrambled over it and sneaked a glance behind her. Way back at the garden gate, she saw the figure of Mike, his head pointing in her direction.

He had seen her.

FIFTEEN

Haunted by a Dark Shadow

Two bars of signal flickered as she reached the stile. Sacrificing valuable seconds, Indigo tried to `phone William but the call failed and she pressed 'Resend' for the text message instead. She tore across the partially frozen muddy field to the forest, her breath puffed in great gasps as cold air ripped at her insides. Wellingtons were not the best footwear to run in, but at that moment she could have sprinted in ski boots. Upon entering the woods, she would try to discover her exact location using Internet maps. However, the police should be able to track her from the text. Thank God she had charged up her `phone.

The barren woods with thousands of skinny white-trunked trees welcomed her into their eerie silence. They swayed back and forth in unison as violent gusts of north wind charged at them. A carpet of brown rotting twigs, leaves and green moss presented a dank surface for the odd flake of snow that wove through the netted tree tops. Stopping for a second, Indigo glanced down at her `phone. The bars had gone back to one but the text message was sent. Indigo sobbed with relief. Then a thought struck her. What if William were oblivious to her absence? A mental picture of him lying asleep with his mouth open came to mind - and then the empty whisky bottle. They may not even be aware of her disappearance.

Mike, although in his fifties, was extremely fit and a regular walker and jogger. Therefore the head start was her only advantage. Scrambling up a crumbling, brown leaf-strewn slope, she spied the sea in the distance and staggered towards the cliffs, praying for physical strength as leg muscles burned with exertion. The sky, a mixture of mauve and beige clouds packed solid with an unbearable weight of ice, dimmed as the light faded. As fat flakes of snow burst from the glacial vapour womb, a ferocious wind whipped them into a frenzy, creating a chaotic blizzard.

Snow landed on Indigo's lips and she crouched for a moment to drink from the water bottle stolen earlier, gulping greedily. It was hours since she'd had any liquid intake. Hastily pulling on scarf, hat and gloves, she zipped up her padded jacket and battled forward. The wind cut into her skin, penetrating her clothing. Visibility was nil, just a relentless wall of flashing white. The wind blasted against her until she was almost vibrating in mid-air. Climbing over a freezing metal six-bar gate, she gazed across the grey swaying ocean. She had reached the coastal path. Hedgerows and cobblestone walls stood between the land and the cliffs. Glancing behind her, she could no longer see Mike due to the weather conditions but she could sense his presence nearby. She ran until her legs lost power and she collapsed onto the path.

Three bars of signal appeared. Sitting she pressed 'My Location' on the map app before bending double and jogging along the path. Her heart hammered in her chest as a griping, clutching sensation squeezed her stomach. Danger was imminent. The ˈphone bleeped and suddenly a flow of text messages appeared from William and Finn; but there was no time to open them. Her location loaded - she was just outside Dunbar. She called William and the ˈphone began to ring.

"Indigo!" He sounded frantic. "Keep your ˈphone on whatever you do. Are you okay?"

The sound of metal clanging in the distance alerted her. Glancing behind, she saw Mike clambering over the gate dressed in his ridiculous, black old-fashioned traveller's cloak with jeans and trainers. Haunted by a dark shadow. Would she ever be free of him? The snowfall eased to a steady pace, adding layer after layer of ice on the ground. The wind chill factor was intolerable and walls of spray escalated up the black slate, shooting up to twenty feet in the air. The sea glinted liquid murky coal in the half-light. Breakers rolled back and forth, threatening to engulf the land in their path.

"Oh God!" she whispered, her teeth banging together. "Near Cockburnspath, nearer Dunbar on the coastal path. He's found me, William!"

Leaving the call live, she scuttled along the path. Powerful blasts of wind blew her into the rocky wall, bashing her tender body. A stile appeared in front of her and she had no option but to climb over it into yet another field that led her away from the cliffs. Microcrystals of ice lit the landscape, crippling her ability to hide but assisting her sight. Hedgerows to the right of her quivered in the wind. Mike dropped back and Indigo prayed that he'd slipped and fallen over the cliff edge or died of a heart attack. Silver prickly barbed wire glinted in the light marking a walkway for ramblers. Dark shadows moved in the dimness and for a moment terror paralysed her; then she realised that the field contained horses. Adrenalin and strength filled Indigo and a surge of energy started in her palms, spreading throughout her entire body.

Behind her a sinister dark presence hunted her as the Egyptian of her dreams had predicted. But she was strong and no victim. Suddenly, deja vu drove a memory into her conscious mind and a cold shiver crept through her as realisation dawned. The nightmare experienced nearly a year ago had become a reality. In the dream, she was being chased through a field at night with horses galloping to the left and hedgerows to the right. As the dream progressed, she'd seen herself in death and devoid of spirit. Her later interpretation of the dream was that the evil creature pursuing her was indicative of Mike and that drastic changes to her life were needed. Her life was valuable and she needed to be aware of her own worth.

Surely the dream hadn't been a premonition? However, the setting of the field, the night and the horses was too much of a coincidence. Indigo didn't believe that coincidences were without significance. They held important information. Since that time, though, Indigo had transformed her life completely. It would make sense if the outcome altered accordingly.

Through a wooden kissing gate, she ventured back out onto the raw coastal path. The next moment, her legs were kicked out from under her and she fell crashing onto her back, winded. Mike straddled her, pinning her arms down at either side of her head. His eyes gleamed with triumph. He was about to take his deserved prize. Remembering William's account of his fight with Mike at the caravan park, Indigo kicked him violently in the back with the heel of her boot. It was enough to dislodge his arms. She punched him viciously in the throat and he fell to the side for a moment, coughing and gasping. As she leapt to her feet, he grabbed her ankle. With her other foot she booted him first in the solar plexus and then in the testicles. Howling and spluttering, he let go of her and she ran. The fight was only victorious because she'd caught him unawares; that wouldn't happen twice.

Mike dived at her legs in a rugby tackle. He had easily out-sprinted her. They rolled over and over, mushing the snow to slush and dangerously close to the cliff's edge. Indigo's head hung over the side and she could make out the sea churning white froth around jagged rocks twenty feet below. Mike slapped her face back and forth. Grabbing his arm with two hands, she bit down on him as hard as she could, drawing blood. Screaming, he leapt to his feet and clutched his bleeding hand.

"Bitch!" he shouted, over the roar of the elements.

Indigo crawled away but he kicked her repeatedly as she curled into a ball, praying to Archangel Michael to intervene. The sky darkened and sleet began to fall. The wind increased in ferocity and Mike staggered backwards towards the cliff edge like a drunk with no co-ordination. Indigo clambered to her feet facing him. Their breath came out in gasps due to the exertion of the battle. Her long dark hair whipped around her face and for a moment she thought she heard voices carried on the wind, but it must have been her imagination.

"You're about to die, Indigo," Mike smiled nastily. "I'm going to throw you off the cliff. They'll all think it was an accident or suicide. Falling twice will look careless." He laughed manically.

"You're mental!" Indigo whispered, partly to herself. 'Help me, Archangel Michael, please." She begged a silent prayer.

A fountain of seawater shot up, soaking them, followed by a barrage of wind that surged and battered them relentlessly. Indigo fell onto her side, pressed to the ground by the forces of nature. Grey, furious gusts pummelled Mike, knocking him back onto his heels. Time slowed down as he toppled backwards. He looked almost comical. Panic and fear registered on his face as his arms circled in an attempt to regain his balance, but the elements overpowered him. He fell onto his back and then over the cliff edge.

Indigo stared at the blank space in the landscape where he had stood. Vomit rose from her stomach and then she heard a shrill screeching.

"Indigo, help me... help me." It came from just below the cliff top.

Shuffling to the brink on her knees, she cautiously peered over. Mike was suspended in mid-air, hanging on to a cluster of roots from an errant bush growing out of the cliff face. Reaching down, she gripped his wrist and pulled him upwards. Snow fell heavily, coating the top of his head and cloak. The shuffle of rapid footsteps sounded behind her, followed by the familiar scent of William's aftershave.

"Indigo... You okay?"

"Mike fell over the edge," she gasped.

Lying next to her on his stomach, William reached down.

"Hold on a second now." Looping a rope around Mike's waist, he instructed Indigo to let go. Finn appeared and helped her into a sitting position. Both men were still dressed in their kilts but with heavy black leather boots, jumpers and coats. Their legs must be frozen, Indigo thought irrationally.

"Are you all right?" demanded William of Indigo, without moving from his position. She nodded and began to cry.

"Just glad you're here... I was so scared." Her voice trembled and she began to shake violently. Finn wrapped the rug he was carrying around her shoulders, pulling her back from the cliff edge.

"There there... You've done well to get away from him. It's okay now. Drink this." He handed her a hip flask full of brandy. As the amber liquid trickled down her throat, warmth spread throughout her body and terror subsided. "What do you want me to do with this joker, Indigo?" William called to her. "Backup's on its way but no here yet - so I'm more than happy to drop him. In fact, it'd be doing me a favour. One less scumbag."

"No!" sobbed Mike in terror. "She pushed me to it - you know what women are like. I'll say I'm sorry. Sorry, Indigo!" he screamed hysterically. Glancing down at the ocean beneath him, he cried like a child. "Please pull me up. I'll do anything!"

William began to laugh.

"You really are pathetic!" he smirked in disgust. "What an excuse for a man you are. You should be flogged and made an example of. Beginning to think death's too good for you."

"You all right?" Finn whispered to Indigo, cuddling her to his chest. The warmth from his body brought relief, but also pain as blood pumped to her many wounds.

"Yeah, I am now... William, he's not worth it. Pull him up."

"You have terrorised and beaten the woman I love." William looked down into Mike's pitiful face. Staring up, Mike whimpered, pleading for his life.

"I'm sorry... I am... Let me make it up to you... I made a mistake. I've said sorry to her!"

William shook his head.

"And what about all the other women? Years ago you would have been sentenced to death by the MacLeod clan of Lewis and burned at the stake - or dropped off the edge of a cliff. And I'm quite old-fashioned." He grinned. "I like the old ways. Plus I'm kinda pissed off that you burned down my house, destroyed my belongings and vandalised my best pal here's Dad's garage. What have you to say?"

"I'll pay for everything, I swear. I was upset... out of my mind. Insane! Please, I have money," he begged. William suddenly loosened the rope and Mike screamed like a girl as he plunged down a few feet. Grabbing the rope, William sat back and hauled him roughly up the cliff onto the snowy grass.

"Thank you, thank you. Whatever you want!" Mike lay gasping and ashen-faced in the light of William's powerful police torch.

"What I want? After everything you did to Indigo, you're now in her debt. You owe her your life. I want to drop you, don't I, Finn?"

Finn nodded.

"He does. He said to me earlier, he would if he got the chance. I'd drop you too." He nodded sincerely. "But she said not to - Indigo's soft-hearted."

"I swear you'll never hear from me again," Mike gushed. Indigo felt embarrassed for him.

"You think I'm gonna let you go?" William's tone was incredulous. "You're going to prison, you eejit," he laughed. "I know quite a few people on the inside so it won't be a pleasant stay, especially if you carry on about your antics against Indigo!"

Renewed panic showed in Mike's eyes. "I won't do anything to her, not now... I said sorry," he squawked. "It's finished, done with."

"On your feet." William hauled him up by the scruff of his neck. His radio crackled. "Back up's two minutes away," he confirmed as Mike stood sheepishly with his head down. Indigo looked at him suspiciously. He was up to something, she was sure.

"William, watch - " she began.

Her warning came too late. Mike kicked William violently in the testicles and fled at speed, cloak billowing out behind him, like a deranged super villain. William knelt on the rope wincing in pain. Taut for a second, it came back to him with a frayed end.

"He has a knife..." Indigo grabbed at Finn who had jumped to his feet. "No, Finn, leave it to the police. William, no!"

Her words evaporated into the darkness as the two men raced after Mike, the beam of William's torch bobbing like a huge yellow orb. Indigo sat for a moment on the cliffs, watching beads of white rushing past her. Sipping brandy, she wrapped the blanket around her shoulders before following their lead. Her body felt sore and stiff but surprisingly strong. Spotting two figures standing in the distance, she realised they were Finn and William. They were standing at the edge of a wide crevice that nature had randomly sculpted out of the land, talking in earnest.

"Did he lose you?" demanded Indigo, beginning to shake.

William shone the beam of light onto the rocks below where the black cloak lay fanned out. Whether Mike was pulp beneath it was a mystery. Indigo's legs gave way and she sank to the ground.

"We didn't kill him, Indigo," William answered her thoughts. "He's quick and lost us. Couldn't understand where he'd disappeared to. Shone the torch about and saw the cloak."

The cloak moved back and forth on the tide.

"He could've flung it there to put us off track but more likely he fell. There's no way he'd have seen the drop, running blind. We only just stopped in time - nearly joined him!" He wiped snow from his long dark eyelashes. "His actions sealed his fate, Indigo. It was his choice to create this vendetta. Don't feel bad for him. He was trying to kill you and you tried to save him. What does that say about you?"

"Er... I'm a mug... a fool... or just stupid? Dunno."

"You're a good person, Indigo," interjected Finn. "I am too. Pity more aren't."

"Don't mention me in that, Findlay," William added dryly.

"You're a policeman, William."

"What's that supposed - "

"Did you see the woman at the cottage?" asked Indigo, interrupting.

"It's empty. No woman or car." William looked at Finn whose face held an unusually blank expression.

"You checked the cellar?"

"Aye, we did. Gathered you've quite a tale to tell, but it can wait until you're rested. We need to get warm before we all get hyperthermia." Torchlight appeared in the distance. "Need to arrange a search party on land and with the coastguard. Doubt they'll be able to do much in this though..." A fountain of sea spray surged upwards. "Visibility not good, rough sea."

Indigo went back to the car with Finn while William spoke to three burly policemen.

"Do you need to go to hospital?" William asked Indigo later as he climbed into the back seat next to her. "He didn't touch you did he? I mean, in that way."

"No, no, thank God - just a bit battered. A mess but it's superficial."

"I'll call the doc anyway. We're going to Wallace's, stay in your old room. Christmas Eve tomorrow..." He took her into his arms. "It's over, Indigo. Dead or alive, after tonight he'll never bother you again." He `phoned the doctor.

SIXTEEN

Indigo Healing

By February, Indigo was the new owner of Fisherman's Watch and the renovation work was well under way. Her superficial injuries, consisting of bruising, scrapes and ripped skin, healed quickly. Her emotional recovery was ongoing, as mood swings of anger, sadness and tearfulness affected her.

Mike's body was never found and the general consensus was that the sea had taken him. The findings of the investigation uncovered empty bank accounts. Mike had transferred all funds to a web of off-shore accounts, weeks prior to his disappearance. Furthermore, he had sold his home in Canterbury through a private agent, unknown to a soul. He had liquidated his assets and run - or that had been his intention. The girlfriend, Catherine from Whitstable, had also disappeared which suggested that they were in it all together.

Despite William's thoughts to the contrary, Indigo felt certain that he was alive. Mike was a proficient sailor and could easily have purchased a boat, sailing it to any destination he chose. That way he could slip into a country undetected, avoiding passport control. He'd mentioned to her that he intended to pursue a new life after obtaining closure. She believed that's what he had done. It was possible that, as his plan unravelled, complications and questions may have arisen causing him to deem it necessary to kill Catherine too. The matter of disposing of her corpse would not be a problem if he had a sailing vessel, since he could store the carcass in the boat and throw it overboard as far away as the Mediterranean. There was a small chance that Mike had fallen into the ravine after all, as William suspected, or that William and Finn had intervened with plans of their own to seal Mike's fate. It seemed she would never know.

William's home was to be rebuilt but he seemed reluctant to live there again, hinting that he would rather share Fisherman's Watch with her. After her recent brush with death, Indigo had a heightened sense of her own mortality; and as she was nearing her mid-forties, saw little point in waiting a few years until it seemed 'appropriate' or sensible to live together. They loved each other and had a tight bond. Their relationship could only improve through time.

Indigo sat on an upturned crate in front of a bonfire sipping green tea with lemon. Orange and purple flames licked the cold air, crackling and hissing, devouring a meal of old rotten floorboards. Finn arrived on his bike, bumping across the field. Indigo pulled a green crate out of the one she was sitting on and poured him a cup of tea from the silver flask.

"Hi. Wow, work's coming along!" He nodded towards Fisherman's Watch that stood opposite, proudly displaying a new grey slate roof.

"Yeah, the builder's great. Really gets things done." She smiled and kissed him on the cheek. "What's that?" Finn held a letter in his hand.

"I sent an email to this guy in Milan with a link to my art portfolio." He beamed with excitement. "He's a businessman with restaurants all over Italy and Europe including London – oh, and a couple in America. And guess what? He wants to commission me to provide paintings for them. Something really chic – different, beautiful but relevant to the restaurants too. It'll mean spending a year at least, painting solidly." He paused to take a sip of tea. "Which reminds me, did you contact that guy who specialises in stained glass? He was reasonably priced and so excited when I mentioned the angel design you wanted."

"I did. He began work a couple of weeks ago. Let me see?" She scanned the letter. "That's brilliant, Finn. It'll be the making of you. Oh, I'm so pleased." She hugged him. "The angels are looking out for us!"

"I know. My idea of Heaven." His handsome face darkened for a second. "Ella was furious, especially when I said I'd return to the monks for six months to paint in Italy, and then here at the studio for the remaining time. I wouldn't have put painting before her if we'd been getting on, or she could've come with me. It's not as if she has some important career or anything to keep her here. Thought she might have been pleased for me."

"Selfish cow," said Indigo crossly. "I'm sorry, Finn. Wish you had a nice girl."

"Not bothered at the moment. Haven't slept together since the ball anyway. I think she's shagging Wallace's pal."

"You're joking!"

"Thought I'd be devastated but I'm not. I was upset to begin with but more hurt pride than anything. I think our relationship ended a long time ago really."

Indigo patted his shoulder sympathetically.

Her `phone bleeped. It was a message from Rebecca, her Reiki Master.

"My Reiki Master's coming to visit in a few weeks so I can complete Reiki Two. She wants to see the house. That will mean I'll be a qualified Reiki practitioner."

"Cool! You'll be able to open the healing centre officially then. That's great." He emptied his cold tea onto the grass. "Dad's all excited because the plans for the North Berwick themed crazy golf course have been approved and they've found someone to put it all together - some firm in Fife that specialises in that sort of thing. All down to you!"

"Glad to help. I've felt useless most of my life - kid's aside. Nice to be appreciated or have something to offer!"

"I can relate to that. I've always felt like that too, a bit of an outcast. But now with the commission... can't believe it! What will you call the Reiki centre?"

"'Indigo Healing'. It'll be similar to the healing retreat on Mull to start with, offering a place of quiet reflection with yoga, Reiki and meditation. Then I'll grow it with the money from Bed and Breakfast. The plan is that in time it'll be similar to Gabriel's healing centre in the Lake District."

"Having a house warming?"

"A small one, just you, William, Wallace and Paula, possibly Rebecca. Oh, and maybe Gabriel and his partner Lana."

◆ ◆ ◆

Two weeks later, the building works were finished to a high standard. The house was yet to be furnished but the refurbishment was complete. Indigo stood outside the new oak front doors with William, Finn and Wallace. The day was sunny and bright with a light breeze.

"Ready for a quick tour?" Inserting a key into the lock, Indigo ushered them inside.

The hallway that had previously been dark and dingy was now bright and full of light due to the vast stained glass window that began at the first stairwell, soaring up to the pitch of the roof and dominating the width of the wall. The seven archangels gazed down upon all who entered, offering solace, protection and love. Archangel Michael, the protector, stood at the forefront of the window, blue rays flowing from the sword held in his hand. He had saved Indigo's life on more than one occasion. He was the original warrior of the light. The remaining six archangels stood behind him creating a V shape. Raphael projected healing rays of green and Jophiel yellow, depicting wisdom and illumination; there was Chamuel's pink aura of love, Gabriel's white light of purity and harmony, Uriel's golden waves of peace and Zadkiel's violet flames of transmutation and freedom. A mosaic had been created at the centre of the V from their colours. The window was artistic, striking and beautiful. Power and energy radiated into the house.

The wooden panelling of the hall had been painted white. Indigo had agonised over the decision but the wood had been too dark and depressing. A sapphire blue marble floor replaced the dirty cracked tiles. The refurbishments to the rest of the house had been minimal. The old French windows had been replaced with a modern equivalent. Fisherman's Watch looked out over the sea and vast picture windows now drew the view into the house; the kitchen wall had been knocked out and a wall of glass peered out over the Bass Rock and May Island. Fireplaces had been buffed and repaired, restored to their formal glory, and wooden floorboards sanded and waxed. Upstairs, modern en-suite bathrooms had been added at the expense of losing one of the six existing bedrooms and splitting the original main bathroom in half.

The main alteration was to the attic that had been transformed into an apartment for rental. It consisted of three bedrooms, all with en-suite bathrooms, a lounge, study, gym, a dining room and a kitchen. Skylights and large rectangular windows brought in light and spectacular views across the bay to Fife. A small lift had been installed as there were numerous stairs to climb and Indigo considered that some of her clients for the healing centre may not be able to manage the ascent.

Walking back down to the lounge, Indigo smiled at the enthusiastic response received.

"That is impressive!" William said. "Really, you've done brilliantly!"

"Class, Indigo," Wallace agreed. "You've done the old place proud!"

"Can't get over the stained glass window - beautiful." Finn hugged Indigo. "Oh, back in a sec..."

Returning with a vast canvas, he leaned it up against the wall. It was portrait and measured around six feet tall by four feet wide. Indigo ripped away the brown paper covering and stepped back to view it properly. Two powerful archangels, Michael and Gabriel, stood naked to the waist with six packs and muscles bared, their intimate parts covered by their rays of blue and white light. Dark cerulean twinkling waters lay behind them and sunshine beamed light upon golden hills in the distance. Their vast wings of silver hugged a beautiful woman with long dark hair and huge indigo eyes, dressed in a simple long white dress, protecting her for eternity. A slow smile crossed Indigo's face as she realised that the woman was her and the faces of the angels were William's and Finn's.

Their laughter was interrupted by William's `phone ringing.

"Seriously though, Finn, that painting is incredible. So powerful! The sort of thing you'd see in the Tate Gallery!" Indigo hugged him.

William disappeared outside to take the call. Walking back into the room moments later, a smug expression covered his face.

"What?" asked Indigo. "William?"

"That was a mate of mine who works for Interpol. He has a friend who works for the Royal Thai Police..." He took a deep breath.

Finn cracked the lids off four bottles of beer and handed them round. Draining half of his, he looked expectantly at William who had paused for effect.

"Get to the point, man," said Wallace impatiently, looking from Finn to William with narrowed eyes. Indigo was baffled. What was going on?

"This friend has just sent him a fax regarding a British national detained for drug smuggling."

Finn's face broke into a huge grin.

"Er, am I being stupid?" said Indigo, looking at Wallace who shrugged. "What's this got to do with us?"

"The Scottish police had alerted the Met and Interpol and others with regards to Mike Cecil Barrington, missing and wanted."

Indigo took a swig of her beer and sat down on the shiny floor. The two men joined her. Wallace perched on a small step ladder.

"You remember, Indigo, when you went to stay at the caravan park and I disappeared on police business? Well, through police contacts, the Internet and friends of mine who are computer experts – well, hackers - we managed to gather a good deal of intelligence on Mike and his future plans." He crossed his legs. "Which was one of the reasons I've been a bit irritable. He's a nasty piece of work even by police standards, and we see the scum of the Earth..." He gulped his beer. "I was aware of him liquidating his assets and transferring funds, also that he'd moored a boat at North Berwick harbour."

"But drugs? Mike? He's so health conscious. Oh my God, he'll get life - or be shot." She looked at William for confirmation. "Isn't drug smuggling death by firing squad?"

William shrugged.

"Doubt it in his case, although it's no more than he deserves. He'll get life, I would imagine," he added confidently. "A British jail would have been too easy for him. Now, Thai jail - that's another matter."

"What about Catherine?"

"Working for an advertising agency in London. Apparently Mike dumped her. My source - good looking guy - took her out for a drink. After several brandies and coke, she confided in him that she and her ex were holidaying in the Borders, first in a lavish house then he'd moved them to this run-down cottage that gave her the creeps. They went for a drink one day and afterwards he put her on a train to Kings Cross and told her to do one – and that she was a boring slapper. He had their bags packed in the boot of the car but didn't return with her. That was the last she saw or heard of him."

"Lovely," commented Wallace, his eyes wide with intrigue.

"She got off lightly!" commented Finn.

"I still can't believe drug smuggling. He's loaded!" Indigo stared at William. "Why would he?"

"How did he make his money, Indigo?" William raised his eyebrows.

"He has legitimate businesses. I know. I did live with him."

"So do the mob! No offence, but you didn't have a clue what he was capable of. Remember your shock when I told you he'd assaulted two other women and been accused of rape?"

"I suppose... But drugs?" Indigo stared at him. "You do have a network of police friends and contacts. Must come in useful."

"It does." He accepted another beer from Finn who was handing out round two.

"Do you have any friends in the Drug Squad?"

He looked vaguely at her.

"Probably. Some move from department to department, but aye."

William would never stand by and let Mike destroy her. He'd told her that. Finn and William had known all the time that Mike hadn't plunged into the ravine and died that snowy night on the cliffs. They had let him run. William had evaluated Mike's character and believed that he would in time renew his campaign of terror against them in the name of revenge. William was a moral man of the law and no murderer. Despite his dramatic utterances, he would never have dropped Mike to his death. Instead, he'd found another way to dispose of him permanently.

"William - you didn't!"

"What?" He looked back at her defiantly, his piercing green eyes full of amusement. "Didn't what?" He laughed down his nose and exchanged glances with Finn.

"You know what! Plant drugs in that boat, knowing he planned to visit Thailand?"

"Indigo!" He pulled her to him, kissing her on the mouth. "What a thing to say! For God's sake, woman, I'm a policeman."

"And as such you fight for justice," she murmured against his lips.

"Exactly. Thy will be done."

If you have enjoyed this book...

Local Legend is committed to publishing the very best spiritual writing, both fiction and non-fiction. You might also enjoy:

A SINGLE PETAL

Oliver Eade (ISBN 978-1-907203-42-8)

Winner of the national Local Legend Spiritual Writing Competition, this page-turner is a novel of murder, politics and passion set in ancient China. Yet its themes of loyalty, commitment and deep love are every bit as relevant for us today as they were in past times. The author is an expert on Chinese culture and history, and his debut adult novel deserves to become a classic.

CELESTIAL AMBULANCE

Ann Matkins (ISBN 978-1-907203-45-9)

A brave and delightful comedy novel. Having died of cancer, Ben wakes up in the afterlife looking forward to a good rest, only to find that everyone is expected to get a job! He becomes the driver of an ambulance (with a mind of her own), rescuing the spirits of others who have died suddenly and delivering them safely home.

JAMIE ON HIS CLOUD

Jaap Rameijer (ISBN 978-1-907203-60-2)

A charming fable of reincarnation for all ages. Against his wishes, Jamie is reborn in first century France with a very special mission. Through his delightful and tragic experiences, we learn about the spiritual purposes of our lives.

THE QUIRKY MEDIUM

Alison Wynne-Ryder (ISBN 978-1-907203-47-3)

Alison is the co-host of the TV show *Rescue Mediums*, in which she puts herself in real danger to free homes of lost and often malicious spirits. Yet she is a most reluctant medium, afraid of ghosts! This is her astonishing autobiography, taking us 'back stage' of the television production.

5P1R1T R3V3L4T10N5

Nigel Peace (ISBN 978-1-907203-14-5)

With descriptions of more than a hundred proven prophetic dreams and many more everyday synchronicities, the author shows us that everyone can receive genuine spiritual guidance for our lives' challenges. World-renowned biologist Dr Rupert Sheldrake has endorsed this book as "...vivid and fascinating... pioneering research..."

SIMPLY SPIRITUAL

Jacqui Rogers (ISBN 978-1-907203-75-6)

The 'spookies' started contacting Jacqui when she was a child and never gave up until, at last, she developed her psychic talents and became the successful international medium she is now. This is a moving account of her difficult life and her triumph over adversity.

Further details and extracts of these and many
other beautiful titles may be seen at
www.local-legend.co.uk

Lightning Source UK Ltd.
Milton Keynes UK
UKOW06f1804260715

255832UK00005B/51/P